Developed to Death

Developed to Death

Rethinking Third World Development

Ted Trainer

GREEN
P R I N T

First published in 1989 by
Green Print
an imprint of The Merlin Press Ltd
10 Malden Road, London NW5 3HR

Reprinted 1994

ISBN: 1 85425 008 6

Text set in 11/12pt Baskerville
by Input Typesetting Ltd
Printed and bound in Great Britain by
Biddles Ltd, Guildford and King's Lynn

Contents

Figures

Tables

CHAPTER 1

The Argument in Outline

What is currently happening in development? Is the Third World developing? Will they make it?

These are among the most urgent questions to be asked in the mid-1980s. Yet there is a remarkable lack of certainty about the answers. We all know things are far from satisfactory, but as to what precisely is wrong and what ought to be done there is considerable doubt and confusion.

This book presents a brief overview and interpretation of the present situation. Its main concern is to suggest a perspective which best enables us to make sense of and evaluate the development scene. This perspective leads to very critical conclusions about what is happening, and to radical implications regarding solutions.

The second chapter sketches the state the Third World is in after thirty years of development effort. Chapter 3 asks about the rate of change: is development occurring and if so at what speed? Although some notable advances in GNP, infant mortality and life expectancy have been achieved, in conventional terms the rate of growth is far too slow to raise the bulk of Third World people to reasonable living standards in a tolerable time span. Even if the rates of growth achieved in the favourable 1950–1970 boom were to continue, this would take hundreds of years. Many indices have deteriorated. Debt has exploded; ecosystems have been depleted; unemployment, urban slums and landlessness have increased. The conclusion arrived at by most of those who have attempted to evaluate development is that the approach that has been taken since World War II has done very little to improve the living standards of the poor majority of the world's people.

The basic assumption underlying the conventional development strategy has proved itself to be invalid. This has been the belief that simply accelerating the rate of growth, the sheer volume of economic turnover, will generate greater national wealth which will then trickle down to raise the living standards of all. What we now know is that very little ever trickles down. Identifying development with sheer economic growth certainly does wonders for GNP, but it does very little for the poor majority. The distribution of national income often becomes worse. Certainly the distribution of world income has become more lopsided. The gap between the few rich countries and the poorest half is increasing fast. The arguments in Chapters 2 and 3 lead to the conclusion that the present approach to development can never solve the problems of the majority of Third World people.

Chapter 4 attempts to explain why development has been unsatisfactory. It begins with a brief summary of the essential elements in the conventional approach to development. It then argues that *most light can be thrown on what is happening by providing an analysis in terms of market forces and the appropriateness of development.* The conventional approach emphatically endorses market forces as the basic factor determining development – it lets the 'law of supply and demand' decide that those who can buy scarce resources or goods which are available for sale are those who can offer most for them, and it lets those with capital set up factories to produce whatever will maximise their incomes. As a direct consequence of this, three highly undesirable effects occur. Firstly, the rich get most of the available resources; secondly, the industries which are developed tend to be those which serve the rich; and thirdly, much of the Third World's productive capacity is drawn into producing for the rich.

There *has* been a great deal of development. *The trouble is that it has been highly inappropriate development.* It has been development in the interests of the rich – the Third World upper classes, the transnational corporations, and the rich countries. The central theme of the book is that market forces have a powerful tendency to produce inappropriate development.

The second half of Chapter 4 re-examines some of the essential elements in conventional development theory in the light of these principles. It gives particular attention to the fundamental mistake of assuming that development necessarily equates with economic growth. Chapter 5 applies the same principles to foreign investment, trade, aid, the International Monetary Fund, and to the food and agriculture problem. Again the argument is that we can best understand what is happening in these areas and what is going wrong if we analyse development in terms of market forces and appropriateness.

The Third World problem is essentially one of deprivation. Probably all poor countries either at present produce enough to meet the basic needs of all their people, or could soon do so given appropriate application of the existing land, labour and capital. Yet a billion people live in appalling conditions, perhaps 730 million are hungry and as many as 80,000 could be dying every day because their basic needs are not met.

Meanwhile the richest fifth of the world's people enjoy a per capita resource consumption about seventeen times the average consumption of the poorest half of the world's people, and GNP per capita about forty-six times as high. They consume four-fifths of the world's annual production of natural resources such as steel, rubber and energy. For anyone concerned about the plight of Third World people the crucial question must be: what produces these extremely unequal distributions? The argument in Chapters 4 and 5 is that the answer is quite simple. They are primarily due to the basic market mechanism built into the foundations of our economic system.

Chapters 2 to 5 attempt to show that it is not at all surprising that conventional development does not work, and that a radically different approach is called for. Chapter 6 introduces a different and much neglected line of argument, but one which comes to the same conclusion. It sketches the 'limits to growth' argument on which a large literature has emerged in the last twenty-five years. The pursuit of affluent living standards and endless economic growth is now generating a number of very serious global problems, notably the destruction of the environment, problems of peace and quality of life, resource scarcity and the 'need' for nuclear energy, as well as the inequality and deprivation evident in the Third World problem. The more we strive to crank-up the level of world production and consumption the more forests and species and soils we will destroy, and the more nations will be drawn into conflicts over access to scarce resources and markets.

A glance at the world's estimated potentially recoverable mineral and energy resources shows that there is no chance of all people rising to the living standards which the few in rich countries have now. The few who live in the 'overdeveloped' countries can only go on enjoying their present resource use if they go on grabbing far more than their fair share. The global economy is therefore grossly unjust. It delivers most of the world's wealth to a few. We who live in the rich countries could not have such high material living standards if the global economy distributed things more evenly. The saying which sums this up is: 'The rich must live more simply so that the poor may simply live'. The overdeveloped countries must eventually face up to a transition to 'conserver' values and systems which enable them to live on something like their fair share of world resources – they must 'de-develop' to a much lower per capita rate of resource use within a zero-growth economy.

All this means that the currently taken-for-granted

supreme goal of Third World development is totally wrong. *The goal of development cannot be to rise to the living standards and industrial-consumer economies which the rich countries now have.* This extremely important point has been almost completely ignored by development theorists of all varieties.

Chapter 7 argues that the unjust global economic system constitutes an empire which enriches a few and deprives many. We in the developed countries could not enjoy such high living standards if we were not drawing wealth from our empire. Three of the mechanisms whereby we do this are the very low wages paid to those who produce things for us in the Third World; our capacity to outbid others in the market for scarce resources; and the huge areas of Third World land which grows things for us when they should be growing things for poor people. These are difficult and controversial issues which oblige us to consider the support which rich countries both East and West give to repressive Third World regimes, and the claim that Western rich countries only give this support to counter 'communist subversion' in the Third World. Chapter 7 argues there are direct connections between the conventional development model, the high living standards enjoyed in rich countries, and the repression carried out by many brutal regimes in the Third World.

Chapter 8 attempts to clarify some of the theoretical issues which are currently the subject of lengthy debate, such as the status of Dependency theory. While tribute is paid to the general value of Marxist social theory, especially in explaining the history of development, it is argued that this theory is insufficient for understanding the current development scene and what is going wrong. In addition it totally fails to come to terms with the 'limits to growth' argument, and this leads to important questions about Marx's ideas concerning the transition to a better social order: do we for example have to wait until capitalism self-destructs, or does the concept of appropriate development point to a more direct and immediate path?

A major concern of the book is to show that we cannot

hope to solve the Third World problem, or the other major and accelerating global problems, unless and until we in the rich countries face up to fundamental social change. Radically different conceptions of development are needed in rich and poor countries alike. These must be framed with the concept of appropriateness centrally in our awareness. Chapter 9 argues that *alternatives do exist*. There is now an extensive literature detailing the abundant scope for appropriate, sustainable, just, ecologically-benign development for rich countries and for poor countries. The central themes are the acceptance of simple material living standards; abandoning the quest for endless economic growth; maximising regional economic self-sufficiency; employing alternative and intermediate technologies; and adopting co-operative ways of working wherever possible.

These alternatives constitute a Third Way. They involve the rejection of the capitalist way with its emphasis on limitless increases in consumption and waste, its disregard for the poor, and its indifference to any concept of appropriate development. They just as emphatically reject the big-state socialist/communist way with its typically central-ised, non-democratic, authoritarian and equally affluence-and-growth-obsessed approach to development. The Third Way is about simple material living standards, local self-sufficiency, grass-roots participation and 'village' democ-racy, living in harmony with the environment, cooperation and zero economic growth. It is also about development defined more in terms of personal, ecological, community and cultural welfare and progress than in terms of the mere accumulation of economic wealth.

The problem is not the lack of alternative ways. We already have all the ideas and examples we need to create very satisfactory material living standards and a high quality of life for all the world's people, on very low rates of consumption of non-renewable resources. The problem is essentially one of bringing people to appreciate the need to abandon the growth and greed society, and more import-antly, to realise that these sustainable alternatives promise a higher quality of life than most people in even the richest countries have now.

Hence Chapter 9 ends with a plea for people to take up the crucial educational task. Our chances of making the transition to a peaceful, just and ecologically sustainable world order depend entirely on whether or not enough of us work hard, perhaps for several decades yet, at helping people to understand the perspective sketched in these chapters, and to see that viable and attractive alternatives do exist.

CHAPTER 2

Conditions in the Third World

Introduction

This chapter offers a brief summary picture of the state of the Third World in the mid-1980s. What is the situation after three or four decades of development effort? Despite some noteworthy achievements the present situation is, to put it mildly, not very satisfactory

Throughout this book I have used the World Bank's basic definitions and categories, although where appropriate other terms have also been used. Thus 'Third World' refers to the two groups labelled by the World Bank as the Less Developed Countries, containing half the world's people, and the Middle Income Countries, containing another quarter of the world's population. This book is mainly concerned with the former group. Table 1 sets out these terms.

ECONOMIC GROWTH

Although a discussion of development should not give too much attention to mere economic growth, I begin with it since it is the main factor which conventional development literature considers.

Table 2 sets out figures on GNP and a number of other basic indicators for 1984. If we take the average 1965–1984

Table 1: Terms

The World Bank's terms	Other terms often used	% of world population
Industrial market economies	Rich western countries; Western developed countries; Rich capitalist countries; First World	16%
East European non-market economies	Rich Eastern countries; Socialist developed countries; Second World	8.5%
Middle Income economies	} Third World	26%
Least developed countries; Fourth World		52%

increase in GNP per capita, the rich western countries (with only one-seventh of the world's people) were increasing their annual per capita incomes by about $270 p.a. in the mid 1980s, while the Low Income Countries (with half the world's people) were increasing theirs by $7 p.a.

But if we take the countries with the poorest 1.3 billion people (i.e., the Fourth World excluding China), where annual incomes have only increased on average .84% p.a. over the 1965–1984 period, we find that the increase averages about $1.90 p.a. in the mid-1980s. Moreover, the distribution of income in these countries is quite uneven. The richest 10% take more than 33% of all income, while the poorest 40% receive around 15%. This indicates that the poorest 520 million in these countries are probably seeing their annual income rise on average by about 73 cents per annum. (This estimate makes the assumption that the poorest groups see their incomes increase at the rate at which the national average increases, which is an unrealistically optimistic assumption.)

In other words, huge numbers of people, the most

Table 2: Major Indicators

	Population (millions, mid-1984)	GNP per capita	GNP Growth Rate % 1965–1984	Life Expectancy (years)	Energy Consumption (Kg oil per capita 1984)	External Public debt \$ (Millions 1984)	Average annual population growth % 1973–1984	Population per doctor 1981
INDUSTRIAL MARKET ECONOMIES (First World, including:)	733.4 (16%)	11,430	2.4	76	4,877	–	0.7	554
USA	237	15,390	1.7	76	7,302	–	1.0	500
Japan	120	10,630	4.7	77	3,135	–	0.9	740
West Germany	61.2	11,130	2.7	75	4,238	–	0.1	420
Australia	15.5	11,740	1.7	76	4,763	–	1.3	500
EAST EUROPEAN NON-MARKET ECONOMIES (Second World, including:)	389.3 (8.5%)	–	–	68	4,360	–	0.8	329
USSR	275	–	–	67	4,627	–	0.9	260
MIDDLE INCOME ECONOMIES (Including:)	1,187.6 (26%)	1,250	3.1	61	743	461,722	2.7	4,764
Indonesia	158.9	540	4.9	55	205	22,883	2.3	11,320
Philippines	53.4	660	2.8	63	271	11,176	2.7	2,150
Brazil	132.6	1,720	4.6	64	753	66,502	2.3	1,200
Mexico	76.8	2,040	2.9	66	1,308	69,007	2.9	1,140

LOW INCOME ECONOMIES (Including:)	2,389.5 (52%)	260	2.8	60	288	72,108	2.0	5,375
Bangladesh	98.1	130	0.6	50	40	5,154	2.5	9,010
India	749.2	260	1.6	56	187	22,403	2.3	2,610
China	1,029.2	310	4.5	69	485	–	1.4	1,730
Kenya	19.6	310	2.1	54	111	2,633	4.0	7,540

Total 4,601.4 m*

*Incl. 16 m in oil exporting countries

(*World Development Report, 1986*, World Bank New York, Oxford University Press, 1986)

desperately needy tenth of the world's people, are actually experiencing no significant increase in their incomes.

RESOURCE USE

More meaningful than comparisons based on GNP and dollar values are statements in terms of the amounts of resources used per capita in rich and poor countries. Figure 1 represents the relative quantities of energy used in various countries. Table 3 sets out some related statistics.

Figure 1: World energy use, 1984

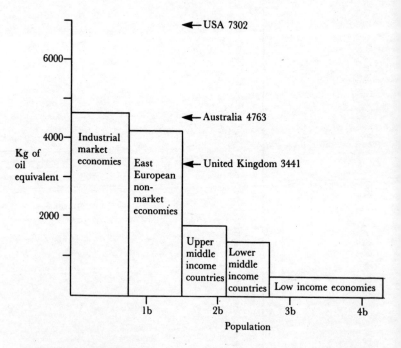

(World Bank, *World Development Report*, New York, Oxford University Press, 1986, pp. 194–195)

Table 3: Inequality in Energy Use

Rich Western Countries average	4877 kg (oil equivalent per capita p.a.)		
Rich Eastern Countries average	4360 kg (oil equivalent per capita p.a.)		
Low Income Countries average	288 kg (oil equivalent per capita p.a.)		
USA average	7302 kg (oil equivalent per capita p.a.)		
Ethiopia average	17 kg (oil equivalent per capita p.a.)		
Ratios:			
Rich Western/Low Income Countries		=	17/1
UK/Low Income Countries		=	12/1
US/Low Income Countries		=	25/1
US/Low Income Countries		=	430/1

(World Bank, *World Development Report*, New York, Oxford University Press, 1986)

The rich countries are consuming over threequarters of the world energy production, yet they only total one quarter of the world's people. Much the same multiple applies to most of the world's scarce resources, such as minerals, timber and fertilizer. If present world energy production were to be shared equally, Americans would have to get by on only one fifth of the per capita amount they presently consume.

These figures pose disturbing questions about the development scene and the way the world economy works. How is it that the few in rich countries are getting far more than their fair share of the world's scarce and dwindling resources? Could our living standards be anywhere near so high if we were not taking most of the world's resource wealth?

THE WIDENING GAP

On some important measures the gap between the rich nations and the poor nations is being closed. Rates for infant mortality, life expectancy and length of life have improved considerably in the Third World in general, while they have remained more or less stable in the rich countries. Much the same applies to ratios of doctors and nurses per person in rich and poor countries.

Yet when it comes to indicators of economc wealth, the gap between the richest and poorest countries is increasing. It has been estimated that two hundred years ago the rich countries had an average income only 1.5 times that of the poor countries.[1] As Figure 2 shows, in 1960 the ratio between the rich western countries and the Fourth World was 20 to 1, and by 1980 it had risen to about 46 to 1.

The world seems to be polarising. About one-fifth of its people are increasing their wealth fairly rapidly, while the poorest fifth did little more than stagnate during the long

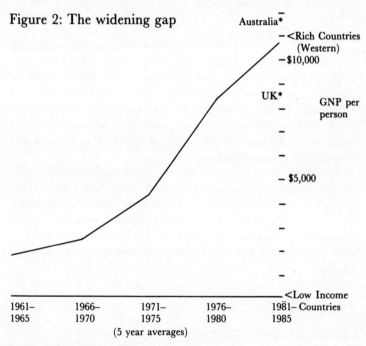

Figure 2: The widening gap

Australia*

− <Rich Countries
(Western)
− $10,000

UK*

GNP per
person

− $5,000

<Low Income

| 1961–
1965 | 1966–
1970 | 1971–
1975 | 1976–
1980 | 1981– Countries
1985 |

(5 year averages)

In 1960 rich average was 20 times poor
In 1980 rich average was 46 times poor

(Derived from *South*, January, 1987, p. 39)

boom, and are now probably becoming poorer in absolute terms. Polarisation is also clearly taking place within some of the richest countries. In the two decades to 1983 the share of wealth owned by the top 10% of Americans rose from 65.1% to 71.7%.[2]

Figures 4, 5 and 6 illustrate this claim quite dramatically. Large increases in national and world wealth have been achieved in recent decades, but they have not been of much benefit to the poorest half of the world's people. It will be argued in Chapter 3 that our economic system has a powerful tendency to focus activity on the already well-off, and either largely ignore the poor or actually deprive them.

It is important not to be misled by the differences in growth rates between rich and poor countries. According to the World Bank the 1965–1984 average rate of growth for the Low Income Countries was 2.8%, compared with 2.4% for the rich Western countries, suggesting that the Third World was actually gaining on the rich countries and would eventually close the gap if these rates continued for a very long time. (Figures from other sources indicate rich countries are growing faster than poor countries.[3]) Over this period, however, *the absolute differences* in dollar incomes was greatly increasing each year. For example, in 1983 the average rich world income rose by about 2.4% of $11,430, or $274, while the average least developed country's income rose by about 2.8% of $260 – only $7. Thus although the rate of increase for the poorest half of the world's people was faster, our dollar increase in income was forty times as great. If we compare the rich western countries with the poorest thousand million people in the world, our annual increase in income in the mid-1980s was *over a hundred times theirs!* If the poorest half of the world's people were to continue to gain on us at this rate of 0.4% p.a., it would take about five hundred years for them to reach the living standards we have now.

As will be emphasised in Chapters 3 and 4, these sorts of figures constitute one of the most forceful arguments against the current approach to development. They show that such an approach requires the Third World to wait generations before satisfactory conditions can be achieved, even though existing productive capacity would permit low but adequate living standards to be provided to all poor people right now, if the necessary redistribution of wealth, resources and power could be carried out.

REAL INCOMES

As the examples in the box below indicate, many people in the Third World have as much difficulty buying necessities for their family as a person in a rich country would have on an income of one-twentieth the present average income. In 1986 the Australian average weekly wage and salary income was over $400. Many Third World weekly incomes would only purchase goods worth $20 in Australian supermarkets. What is more, the income is often available only for short periods. When the main work in the sugar plantations is over for the season, for example, the labourers become unemployed.

Real Incomes

Domitala, wife of a Bolivian tin miner, makes and sells pies to earn about 20 pesos a day. Meat costs 28 pesos a kilo. Her husband earns 28 pesos a day.

'Let me speak', *Monthly Review*, Feb. 1979, p. 43.
In Bangladesh a landless labourer earns two pounds of rice, 7 cents and a meal for a day's work. The 7 cents buy less than 1 lb of rice. 'When Sharifa can find work husking rice she usually receives only a pound of rice for a day's labour.'

B. Hartmann and J. Boyce, *Needless Hunger*, IDFP, 1979, pp. 27, 32.
'Abdul Malek is a landless labourer in Bangladesh who has to leave home every morning to search for work for the day ahead. If he succeeds he will be able

to buy about two pounds of rice with his day's wage, although he himself will have to eat about a pound of this to be strong enough to continue working. So, even on a good day there is not much to share with his family. If nobody wants him to work there will be almost nothing for any of them.' (In Australia in 1979, two pounds of rice cost about $1.50; try feeding your family on $9 per week.)

From *The New Internationalist*, Nov. 1979.

'In Accra, the impoverished majority . . . must spend three days' wages for a kilo of meat, and one day's wages for a tin of condensed milk or a kilo of fish or poultry. Even on the rare occasions when they are available, sugar, flour, tinned fish, and soap are beyond an unskilled worker's income.'

R. Fuller, *Inflation*, Worldwatch Paper 34, Jan. 1980, p. 12.

LANDLESSNESS

There were very few landless rural families in Asia thirty years ago. In many regions over a third of rural people are now landless. In Latin America 11% were landless in 1961, but by 1975 40% were.[4] The accelerating rate at which people have become landless is one of the Third World's most serious problems. It generates other major problems, notably the rapid growth of urban slums as people migrate from the country in search of jobs. One of the main criticisms of the conventional approach to development is that it creates these problems by 'modernising' agriculture in ways that benefit a few while squeezing large numbers off the land (see Chapter 4). The landlessness problem is partly due to population growth, but it is primarily due to the failure to develop in ways that would provide jobs for all rural people. Approximately 80% of all Third World agricultural land continues to be owned by about 3% of landowners.[5] As Chapter 4 will make clear, most Third

World development constitutes development of the wrong things – it is not development of those industries which would enable people to stay in rural areas and be usefully employed there.

HEALTH

A large proportion of Third World people endure appalling health conditions. Hundreds of millions suffer easily curable or preventable illnesses. The Low Income Countries average 5,375 people per doctor and 3,920 per nurse. In the Industrial Market countries the figures are 554 and 177, indicating that access to medical personnel is about fifteen times as good in rich countries. Many millions have no access at all, especially those who are too poor to pay for medical treatment.

The world's single biggest health problem is lack of clean water. This could be seriously endangering the lives of more than a billion people, and for many more it is a considerable problem. It is probably responsible for more than 25,000 deaths every day caused by diseases carried in unsafe water. Poor villagers cannot afford pipes and sewer systems, partly because the materials that could go into the production of these facilities go into cars and video recorders for the rich fifth of the world's people.

Dangerous Water

'Probably the majority of the people in the developing countries use domestic water from sources that are subject to contamination.' ... 'In 5 villages from widely separated parts of India it was found that from 23% to 75% of the people were infected with roundworms, hook worms, pin worms, dwarf tapeworms and intestinal amoebas. Many villagers are sick a good deal of the time. They are unable to absorb all the food they eat because of the damage done by

parasites to the intestinal membranes and because part of their food goes to feed the worms and protozoa that infest their intestines.'
> *The Population Debate*, UN Dept. of Social and Economic Affairs, 1975, p. 100.

'We know of cities in Latin America where 60% of the children are dead before they are 5 years old, of diseases bred by filthy water . . .'
> *Water and Children*, UNICEF News, 91, 1977.

'Over 80% of all illness in the developing world is directly or indirectly associated with a poor water supply and sanitation.' In Ethiopia only 1% of the people have safe water. '. . . one sixth of all African children die before their first birthday in a normal year'.
> L. Timberlake, *Africa in Crisis*, London, Earthscan, 1985, pp. 48, 15.

In Africa, boys may be seen leading a number of adults, each holding onto the one piece of rope or a branch, because they have lost their sight to river blindness or some other waterborne parasite. A food intake too low to provide sufficient Vitamin A, almost never a problem in the rich countries, results in perhaps one hundred thousand Third World children losing their sight every year.[6]

URBAN BIAS

The small middle class, the tiny rich class, and the urban workers carry much more political weight than the majority who live in the countryside.

The government, including the bureaucracy, is usually made up entirely of people from the middle and the rich classes. Consequently government policies often tend to favour the urban groups while neglecting rural groups, and to siphon wealth from rural to urban regions (for example, by setting low prices for agricultural produce). Lipton's influential argument[7] has been that this urban bias explains the underdevelopment experienced by the majority of Third World people. However, it could be argued that urban bias occurs because it suits the most wealthy and powerful few in the world, especially the transnational corporations, to focus development on the rich few in the Third World and to ignore the poor; thus urban bias could be a consequence of the *real cause* of underdevelopment.

UNEMPLOYMENT AND UNDEREMPLOYMENT

In western Third World countries, unemployment and underemployment are huge problems. Often the numbers completely unemployed are not so large because in the absence of unemployment pensions people must find some way of earning some money; but this just means that large numbers of 'workers' spend much of their time without earning. For example, a person might set up as a shoeshine boy, but find only ten customers all day. The number unemployed and underemployed in the Third World could add to the equivalent of 300 million totally unemployed. The unemployment rate may be in the region of 30%.[8] Because of future population increase, several hundred million more jobs will be needed in coming decades. This is one of the most critical challenges to the present approach to development. It has little chance of providing jobs and reasonable incomes to such numbers.

NATURAL DISASTERS

> 'In the 1970s six times as many people died from natural disasters as in the 1960s. In the 1960s floods affected 5.2 million people p.a.; in the 1970s, 15.4 million.'
>
> L. Timberlake, *Africa in Crisis*, Earthscan, 1985, p. 20.

Why have 'natural' disaster tolls been rising?

Firstly, increasing numbers of very poor people are forced to live in dangerous areas, such as deltas liable to flooding and in houses built on stilts over tidal flats where typhoons rage. Secondly, the impact of floods and droughts has been increased by the deterioration of ecosystems. For instance, less forest means more sudden rain run-off, more floods and more severe droughts. This is a factor likely to have an accelerating impact on the real living standards of the Fourth World because ecological systems are being damaged at such an alarming rate.

THE FOOD AND HUNGER PROBLEM

Several hundred million people in the Third World are hungry. Estimates vary, and even slight variations in assumptions about minimum food requirements make considerable differences to the figures, but at least 350 million people do not receive sufficient nutrition. One study arrived at a figure three times as high.[9] In the later 1970s the UN estimated that 730 million people were inadequately nourished.[10]

The food situation in Latin America and Africa has probably deteriorated since 1980.[11] Grain production per capita is falling in no fewer than forty Fourth World countries.[12] Five to ten million people are estimated to die directly or indirectly from insufficient food each year.[13]

Figure 3 shows that on average food production in the poor countries has just kept ahead of population growth. The overall gain in the 1970s was negligible.[14] African production is the most disturbing, having steadily fallen behind population growth. In 1980 African per capita food production was 15% below the 1960 level.[15] Note that these figures include production of crops for export, which are often increasing twice as fast as crops for local consumption, so they probably significantly overestimate the rate of growth of food per capita for local people to eat.

Figure 3: Indices of Third World Food-Production

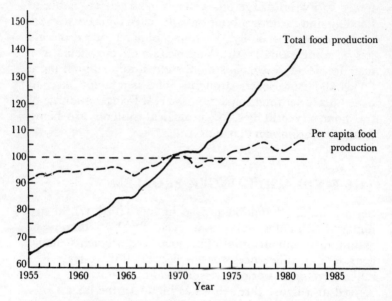

(from M. P. Todaro, *Economic Development in the Third World*, New York, Longmans, 1985, p. 289)

The Extent of the Hunger Problem

The low estimate of the number of starving to death each year is 10–15 million.
R. McGutcheon, *Limits of a Modern World*, 1979, p. 39.
'4 out of every 5 babies born in the developing countries face the horrors of hunger and malnutrition. 2 out of every 5 die before reaching their fifth birthday.'
Dr. A. H. Boerma, Director of F.A.O., quoted

in *Development Handbook*, Freedom From Hunger
Campaign, 1982, p. 36.
In 1978 UNICEF '. . . estimated that . . . more than
12 million children under the age of five died of
hunger.'
W. Brandt, *North South*, 1980, p. 16.
The World Bank estimates that there are 1 billion
people chronically malnourished.
Editorial, *Science*, 27th June, 1980, 208, 4451.
Starvation kills 18¼ million people every year. 1,000
million are hungry.
United Nations, *Development Issue Paper for the
1980's, II; Food*, p. 2.

IS THERE TOO LITTLE FOOD PRODUCED?

The world produces much more than enough food to
provide for the needs of all people. There is sufficient grain
alone produced to meet all needs. Most if not all Third
World countries produce sufficient food for their own
needs, or could do so if access to land and other food
producing resources were more evenly distributed.
Murdoch[16] states that all could feed themselves.

IS THERE TOO LITTLE LAND?

The food and hunger problem cannot be explained by
insufficient crop land per person. Many of the poorest
countries have more land per person than many rich European countries. India has over four times as much arable
land per person as Japan (see Table 4).[17] The difference is
that rich countries can afford to import much of their food,
and to buy large quantities of energy to invest in food
production. Poor people in the Third World cannot afford
to buy the available food, or do not have access to the land
on which they could produce it. In other words, *people are
hungry because they are poor, not because there is insufficient food*

or land available. Even in times of famine there is often quite enough food within the country in which people are starving to death. Deprivation is nearly always a matter of unsatisfactory distribution and insufficient 'effective demand' – the inability to buy what is available. Consequently, the basic solution to the food and hunger problem is not to increase production; it is to increase the ability of poor people to buy food, and to produce it for themselves.

Table 4: Too little land per person?

Country	Hectares of arable land per capita
Japan	.05
United Kingdom	.13
Bangladesh	.13
Indonesia	.15
Philippines	.23
India	.30
Thailand	.32
Pakistan	.40

(W. Murdoch, *The Poverty of Nations*, Baltimore, Johns Hopkins University Press, 1980, p.187)

NEW SOURCES OF LAND?

The amount of land in the world that could potentially be cultivated is about twice as much as is currently being used. However, it will be increasingly costly to bring the additional land into production as it is less fertile and in more difficult locations, meaning that the food produced from it will be more costly and could therefore be too expensive for poor people to buy.

In addition, the world is losing large areas of cropland every year through environmental deterioration, especially erosion. Some people have estimated that in the twenty years between 1980 and 2000 we could lose as much as a third of the area presently in use, meaning no net increase in the area cultivated.[18]

YIELD INCREASES

Increases in food production are likely to continue to be due much more to improving yields than increasing the area of land under cultivation. There is considerable room for improvement, but in general yields in the developed countries are not vastly greater than those in the Third World. For example, India achieves about 2 tonnes of rice per hectare compared with 5.5 tonnes per hectare in the USA, despite the fact that the US fertiliser use per arable hectare is three times the Indian amount.[19] This multiple is fairly characteristic of rich and poor nation grain yields.[20] To assume that the Third World could rise towards yields achieved in the developed countries is to assume that poor countries can afford the large amounts of costly inputs that would be required. Irrigation, mechanisation, pesticides, fertilisers and storage all require expensive energy and resources.

Yield increases in the rich countries have now tended to level off, and in several important cases, notably grains, long term trends in absolute yields per hectare appear to have begun to fall recently.[21] This is partly because poorer land is being introduced.

It should not therefore be assumed that it will be easy for the Third World to achieve remarkable increases in yields in future years. There is in fact considerable evidence of falling yields within the hungriest parts of the Third World. In four large African countries 1980 yields were lower than in 1950, due partly to erosion.[22] Growth of irrigated areas has slowed to a negligible rate. The US irrigated area has actually decreased due to rising pumping costs and water depletion.[23]

THIRD WORLD FOOD IMPORTS

There has been a strong trend towards increasing imports of food into the Third World in the last two decades. Concern has been expressed about how much further the import curve can rise. Will debt-ridden poor countries be able to afford increasing amounts? Will rich countries have increasing amounts of food available for sale? Both the USA and the USSR have recently made significant reductions in their grain areas, having realised they were pushing marginal land too hard.[24]

'In 1970 Africa fed itself. In 1980 the equivalent of its entire urban population was being fed on imported grain. By 1984, 140 million of the total 531 million were being fed on imported grain.'
    L. Timberlake, *Africa in Crisis*, Earthscan, 1985, p. 67.

FOOD PROSPECTS

It is difficult to be at all certain about the future of the food problem. Technical improvements are likely to continue to be achieved, but some important factors are likely to deteriorate. Especially important is the apparently accelerating destruction of Third World ecosystems, seriously undermining the future productivity of agriculture. Huge losses of forests and soil are occurring, overgrazing is increasing, and fallow periods are being shortened. As forest loss accelerates, the soil's capacity to hold water declines and so rain runs off quickly, causing erosion, droughts and floods, and the silting up of dams. Forests hold water and enable it to soak into the ground, ensuring much longer run-off periods and thereby keeping streams running more constantly. As the forests decline, fuel wood becomes more scarce and peasants burn more dung, reducing the volume of nutrients being returned to the soil.

Population growth, especially the conversion of the best lands to export cropping, has meant that poor people are increasingly obliged to move onto more fragile lands and to overgraze them. Consequently when heavy rains or droughts occur there is much more devastation than would otherwise have occurred. Meanwhile rising debt problems of Third World countries are leaving them less able to devote resources to remedying these environmental problems.

Some have likened these deteriorating conditions in Third World environments to a biological time bomb that will explode in coming decades. In many parts of Africa the trends have already had catastrophic effects on millions of people. In 28 of the 38 African countries the rate of growth of food production was lower in the 1970–1982 period than in the 1960s.[25]

In addition to these environmental problems, the costs of inputs such as fertiliser and energy are likely to rise in the long term, unit returns on agricultural inputs are diminishing, and there is increasing difficulty over access to sufficient water. World grain stocks have fallen in the long term, pointing to declining capacity of the rich world to supply Third World demand. The increasing debt problem is reducing the Third World's capacity to import grain.

Meanwhile the numbers to be fed are growing. World grain production will have to increase 26% in the next thirteen years just to sustain present per capita levels, and 56% by 2020.[26] Yet world cropland per person fell from 0.25 ha in 1950 to 0.15 ha in 1980.[27]

Some authors are relatively optimistic about food prospects, although the optimists tend to focus on what might be achieved with moderate increases in inputs or with various policy changes, without much thought as to whether such changes are likely to be made in view of current economic forces and power structures. The outlook is uncertain, but there are clearly reasons for serious concern.

'The 1970s and the early 1980s also witnessed a transition from a previous era of commercial food
surpluses to one of global shortages, rising prices, and
growing national concern. . . .'

M. P. Todaro, *Economic Development in the Third
World*, New York, Longmans, 1985, p. 544.

THE POPULATION PROBLEM

Many Third World countries have high rates of population
growth, and it is often assumed by people unfamiliar with
development literature that most of their difficulties are
simply due to too many people. Population growth is
without doubt a major global problem, and growth rates
in a number of poor countries are disturbingly high. Population growth alone, however, is far from a sufficient explanation for Third World problems.

Figures showing the amount of land per person indicate
that the most overpopulated countries in the world are the
rich countries; most of the countries where hunger is a
problem have much more farm land per person than Japan
or Europe. Hunger cannot therefore simply be explained
in terms of too many people in relation to land or food
production.

The explanation which is now widely accepted is that
in general rapid population growth rates are the *result* of
underdevelopment, not its cause. The main reason why
people in the Third World have many children is because
they are poor. In other words, when you understand the
economic conditions they have to live under, you realise
why it is important for them to have large families. If there
are no pensions then a person's only chance of being looked
after when he or she is old is to have surviving children,
and if the infant mortality rate is high then people must
have many children to be sure that some will survive. In
addition, the more children a peasant has the more labour

there is available to work the farm. A five year old child can be a useful worker on a family farm.

Often birth control programmes are quite effective, but not if they are introduced in situations where economic conditions provide a powerful incentive for having large families. It is now widely agreed that the most effective way to solve the problem of rapid population growth in poor countries is to achieve satisfactory development – to reduce poverty and infant mortality, and to rise to levels of national wealth where water can be piped to villages and pensions can be provided. When people are more economically secure they will not feel such a need to have large families. As Murdoch says in summarising his extensive discussion of the issue, '. . . the solution to the population problem is to increase the level of economic well being of the vast majority of families'.[28]

> '. . . children provide one of the few sources of economic and social security in old age for very poor families.'
> M. P. Todaro, *Economic Development in the Third World*, New York, Longmans, 1985, p. 89.

A DEMOGRAPHIC TRAP?

In the early 1980s it became apparant that many countries might fail to complete the 'demographic transition' from high to low birth and death rates, mainly because of the destructive impact of rapidly increasing numbers on ecosystems and economic support systems. When the transition begins, death rates fall first, leading to higher population numbers and therefore to a race between the increasing numbers and the development needed to provide for them. If satisfactory development is as elusive for large numbers as this book argues, it is quite possible that many countries will fail to complete the transition.

Brown estimates that perhaps half the world's people might soon be in this situation.[29] He believes that we have now polarised into a half with 1% p.a. population growth, and another half averaging 2.2%.

PROJECTED WORLD POPULATION

Present projections indicate that world population will rise from 5 billion in 1987 to stabilise in the period 2050–2100 at around 10–11 billion. People then living in what are now Third World countries will probably number about 8½ to 9 billion. The developed countries are increasing their numbers very slowly, so most of the increase in world population will take place in Third World countries. This means that after 2050 the population of the presently poor countries will probably outnumber that of the presently rich countries by 6 or 8 to 1.

Because a large proportion of people in poor countries are relatively young, and will be having children and grandchildren before their parents die, there is a great deal of 'inertia' in the population growth rate of many countries. For example, India now has around 700 million people, but its population is unlikely to stabilise below 2000 million late next century even if very effective birth control programmes are introduced quickly. Even the lowest probable population growth rates will mean quite serious additional demands on the world's already scarce and expensive resources, and especially on its ecosystems.

THE DEPRIVATION TOLL

The essential issue in the development story is the gross maldistribution of world wealth and productive capacity. Most people in the world are deprived of things they can and should have. For about a fifth of the world's people this means shortage of the goods and services without which life is very difficult, and is often endangered. It is possible that a fifth or more of the world's people are too poor even to feed themselves adequately. At least the billion people in the poorest half of the Fourth World are so deprived of access to basic necessities that they suffer tens of thousands of otherwise avoidable deaths every day. Dammann concludes that 82,000 people die every day because they cannot secure adequate food and other resources.[30] For the past several years UNICEF has announced that the death toll among the world's children is in excess of 40,000 every day. Hunger probably kills more than five million people every year. Contaminated drinking water probably kills another five to ten million. The immediate cause of these deaths is usually an illness, but the real cause is the lack of food or clean water which could have been remedied had there been greater access to basic resources.

Thus there could be up to thirty million avoidable deaths every year. The main argument in this book is that this disaster, equal to 160 fully loaded jumbo jets crashing every day, is almost entirely due to a grossly unjust global economic system.

THE DEBT SITUATION

Table 5 shows how steeply the Third World's total debt has risen in recent years. In 1987 it was in excess of $1000 billion, and debt service was costing the Third World $135 billion every year.[31] Most of the debt is held by a small number of more developed Third World countries, but many more have quite high debt in relation to their export earnings or their GNP. By the mid-1980s the total debt had risen to the point where it was feared that the most heavily indebted rich world banks might collapse, triggering a serious worldwise depression.

The problem has been due partly to over-enthusiastic lending by banks holding abundant funds after the oil price rises of the early 1970s, partly to the slump in global economic activity since then and the associated fall in Third World export earnings, and partly to the high interest rates of the early 1980s. In other words, the

Table 5: Debt

Indicator	1980	1981	1982	1983	1984	1985
Ratio of debt to GNP	21.1	22.8	26.8	31.8	32.7	33.0
Ratio of debt to exports	90.1	97.5	116.4	134.3	130.4	135.7
Debt service ratio	16.1	17.7	20.7	19.4	19.8	21.9
Ratio of debt service to GNP	3.8	4.1	4.7	4.6	5.0	5.3
Ratio of interest service to exports	7.0	8.3	10.4	10.0	10.5	11.0
Total debt outstanding and disbursed (billions of dollars)	431.6	492.5	552.4	629.9	674.1	711.2

(World Bank, *World Development Report*, New York, Oxford University Press, 1986, p. 32)

problem has been due mostly to factors outside the control of the Third World.

The terms of repayment for some of the biggest debtors were rearranged a number of times during the 1980s. These moves managed to avoid major defaults, but they only deferred problems rather than solved them. There is no realistic chance of most of the debt ever being repaid. At some point in the future governments in the rich countries will probably help their banks to write off most of the debt in order to save the world from a major depression.

The debt situation can be seen as another good reason for rejecting the conventional approach to development. It is difficult to believe that an approach which has seen the explosion of debt is ever likely to lead the Third World to prosperous, self-sustaining growth.

'Africa's debt burden is now intolerable', said Tanzanian President Julius Nyerere more bluntly in London in early 1985. 'We cannot pay. You know it and all our other creditors know it. It is not a rhetorical question when I ask, should we really let our people starve so that we can pay our debts?'

L. Timberlake, *Africa in Crisis*, Earthscan, 1985, p. 34.

INEQUALITY, PRIVILEGE, DEPRIVATION AND EXPLOITATION

In Third World countries there tend to be greater differences between people in income, wealth and power than there are in developed countries. In many countries the rich few oppose and exploit the poor majority, by paying them very low wages for work in plantations and factories, and by using the law, the police and the army to force people to accept their conditions. In many cases the poor majority could, if they had access to land, produce for themselves many of the basic things they need, especially food, but the rich few will not permit this. In Latin America the big landowners often keep most of their land idle and thereby prevent poor people from cultivating it to grow food for themselves. This ensures that the poor are willing to accept work in the plantations for low wages.

Inequalities in Wealth and Power

In El Salvador in 1979, 2% of the total population owned 60% of the arable land.
New York Times Weekly Review, 9th March, 1980.
According to the U.N. Food and Agriculture Organisation, 1.3% of landowners in Latin America have 71.6% of cultivated land.
M. P. Todaro, *Economic Development in the Third World*, New York, Longmans, 1985, p. 295.

There is considerable agreement that the basic problem in the Third World is not a shortage of food or other resources and wealth, but the very uneven and unjust distribution of the existing resources and wealth, especially land. It is most unlikely that any significant improvement in the living standards of the poor majority can be achieved unless these unjust and repressive social conditions are changed.

Treatment of the peasants in Paraguay: 'The police beat them up as soon as they try to organise themselves. They have no rights at all, not even the right to protest.' The Catholic Church has been trying to get peasants to form producer cooperatives. 'One day soldiers arrived, beat up the peasants, tied them up and took them off in trucks. Last May they destroyed the cooperative warehouse and took away the produce.' ... 'Twenty companies controlled by foreign capital own 30% of the land in Paraguay ... the companies controlled by foreign capital are responsible for over 80% of Paraguayan exports.'

The Guardian, February 27, 1977, p. 12.

'Hundreds of thousands of poor Guatemalans have been pushed off their farmlands over the last 30 years by wealthy landowners seeking high profits from export crops. Today, the richest 2% of landowning families control 80% of the country's farmland.'

'Deprived of enough land to grow food, they are forced to take the only work available – two or three months a year harvesting coffee, cotton and sugar cane to be shipped to well-fed people thousands of miles away. Their pay: $2 a day or less. No wonder the poorest 50% of Guatemalans – mainly Indians – get only a little more than half the calories that they need. No wonder hunger-related diseases kill *half* of their children before they reach the age of five.'

'In the last five years alone, over 10,000 civilians have been killed ... Why? To keep control of the country and its resources in the hands of the Army and a wealthy elite, both backed by the U.S. government and U.S. investors.'

Guatemala: Hungry for Change. Food First Action Alert, March 1983.

'The richest 1% of Haitians monopolize 44% of the nation's income. As for the other 5 million Haitians, the World Bank estimates that 80% survive on about

$100 a year. Some of those lucky enough to have jobs work for the more than 250 U.S. Companies assembling baseballs, electronics and clothing – all for export. The usual wage is $2.64 a day (33 cents an hour) and unions are banned. Large landowners control the best land, mainly used for export crops, including sugar, cotton and coffee. Poor Haitians have been forced onto marginal lands on mountainous slopes.'

Haiti, Food First News, Summer, 1983.

Peasant farmers in Thailand sometimes have to pay interest of more than 100% per month, on loans. Trade unions and strikes are outlawed.

P. de Beer, 'Thailand's chaotic economy', *The Guardian*, 28 Aug. 1977.

'In many countries tenants have to hand over to the landlord 50–60 percent of their crop as rent . . .'

S. George, *How the Other Half Dies*, 1976.

MEANWHILE, IN THE OVER-DEVELOPED COUNTRIES

It is important that we should compare the conditions that most people in the world experience with those enjoyed by the very few very privileged people in the world. After all, the essence of the Third World problem is the grossly uneven distribution of the world's wealth. Bearing in mind that most of the world's people experience the impoverished conditions sketched in the previous pages, consider some of the taken-for-granted extravagance, luxury and waste characteristic of the lifestyles of most people who live in the over-developed countries.

Americans put more fertilizer on their lawns and tennis courts than India uses for all purposes.

New York Times, 14th June, 1979.

In 1975 Americans spent $4,300 million on barber shop, beauty and bath services.

> P. Harrison, *Inside the Third World*, 1979. p. 361.

Australians drink an average of 65 litres of soft drink every year.

> *National Times*, Sept. 14–20, 1980, p. 37.

Australians own 4,139,000 dogs. $180 million is spent on pet food every year.

> *Sydney Morning Herald*, Feb. 25th, 1980; *Choice*, Sept. 1980.

The Japanese sent 22 billion New Year cards at the end of 1978.

> *Sydney Morning Herald*, 5th Jan. 1979.

Australians have $100 million worth of air conditioners in their cars.

> *National Times*, 16th Dec. 1978, p. 58.

In the 1950s Americans spent $5,339 million every year just to change their car models.

> F. Fisher et al. 'The costs of automobile model changes since 1949', *Journal of Political Economy*, Oct. 1962.

In 1986 Australia imported $152 million worth of beverages, $1,154 million worth of cars, and $84 million worth of caviar.

> *Sydney Morning Herald*, 16th May, 1986, p. 4.

There are between 12 and 20 electric motors in the average American kitchen.

> A.B.C. Radio, *Technology Report*, 8th April, 1987.

America produced, and threw away, 88,000,000,000 tin cans in 1981.

> U.S. Bureau of Mines, June, 1983.

The essential task for development educators is to help people in over-developed countries to understand that their affluence is intimately related to the poverty of most of the world's people, and that it will never be possible for all people to live as affluently, or to consume as much, as people in the over-developed countries do now.

We live on islands of affluence in a sea of poverty.

CONCLUSIONS

It can be argued that only about one-sixth of the world's people live fairly comfortably or better. The poorest 40%, around two thousand million people, live in very difficult circumstances, and half of these people endure extreme poverty and a range of associated problems such as illness, squalor, exploitation, violence and hunger. Perhaps a thousand million are malnourished. For one reason or another perhaps as many as 80,000 die unnecessarily every day, simply because they do not have access to the available and sufficient resources.

In other words, the state of development is very unsatisfactory. This might be more tolerable if we could see that the situation was improving rapidly, or at least if we could see that the development effort was on the right track and would in time solve the problems. The next two chapters take up these questions.

CHAPTER 3

Is Development Occurring?

Chapter 2 summarised the disturbing conditions that most of the world's people have to endure. The situation prompts the very important question: 'How fast are things improving?' There are certainly areas of unambiguous improvement, but many other issues lead to the inevitable conclusion that satisfactory development is emphatically not occurring. A great deal of development is taking place, but it is not satisfactory development and it is most unlikely ever to solve the problems of the majority of people.

THE GAINS

Let us begin again with GNP, since this is taken by conventional economists to be the overwhelmingly important indicator of development. In the post war period, GNP per capita in the Third World has grown at a rapid rate, not very different from that of the developed countries, and much faster than the growth in the latter countries when they were beginning to develop. World Bank figures indicate an average of 2.8% p.a. growth from 1965 to 1984, compared with 2.4% for the rich countries,[32] though other sources give less favourable figures: UNICEF for example gives 2.1% for the Third World and 2.7% for the rich countries in 1986.[33] As is discussed below, growth rates in the 1980s have fallen, and have been negative in a number of countries.

Even if attention is confined to achievements during the highly favourable 1950–1970 'long boom', in per capita terms the least developed countries' rate of growth was far too slow to produce satisfactory effects within a reasonable time. In Chapter 2 it was stated that the average rate of increase in income in the two decades to 1985 for the poorest half of the world's people has been around $7. The few World Bank figures available[34] indicate that half of the Third World's income goes to the richest fifth, and that the poorest two-fifths receive about 15%. This suggests that the world's poorest 520 million people average annual incomes of $87, and that over the twenty years of the boom these incomes increased only by an average of 73 cents p.a.

If we take the 28 poorest countries, excluding China, containing 30% of the world's people, per capita growth between 1965 and 1984 averaged only 0.85% p.a. At this rate it would take these countries over three hundred years to rise from their present $222 per capita average income to just *half* of the *present* average for the rich Western countries. To use figures from the post 1980 period of slower growth would be to arrive at far more disturbing conclusions.

Even if the growth rate of the poor countries doubled, only 7 would close the gap with the rich nations in 100 years. Only another 9 would reach our level in 1000 years.

> Robert McNamara, ex-president of the World Bank, quoted by A. G. Frank, 'World system in crisis', in W. R. Thompson, Ed., *Contending Approaches to World Systems Analysis*, London, Sage, 1983, p. 29.

Meanwhile, remember that each year the average

income in the rich Western countries increases about forty times as much as the average income for the poorest half of the world's people, and that whereas the ratio of these two incomes was about 20 to 1 in 1960 it reached about 46 to 1 in 1980.

Most if not all poor countries have sufficient resources and productive capacity to provide all their people with very modest but adequate living standards. An approach to development obliging the most urgently needy billion to wait generations and even centuries for significant improvements in their material living standards is clearly unacceptable.

LIFE EXPECTANCY, INFANT MORTALITY AND LITERACY

Achievements in these three areas constitute the most impressive elements in the case for the conventional approach. Third World life expectancy in 1950 was around 35 years, but in 1981 had risen to approximately 58 years.[35] Infant mortality fell from 164 per 1000 to 90 in the same period.[36] Morawetz[37] notes that gains in mortality have been in part due to campaigns against infectious disease, such as the eradication of smallpox. In addition, given that distributions of wealth and welfare in the Third World are very uneven, it is quite likely that the improvements in average rates for these factors have been due more to gains by the relatively privileged sectors and that achievements for the poor majority have been considerably lower.

There is evidence that the rate of improvement in these factors had started to level off even before the onset of the 1980s downturn in the global economy.[38] The anecdotal reports (summarised in Table 6) indicate that in many regions no gains are occurring in the 1980s, and there have even been some reversals.

DEBT

Far from progressing towards self-sustaining economic growth and prosperity, the Third World has fallen into such levels of debt that few now hold any hope for repayment, and many fear for the safety of the entire global economic system.

THE 1980s

There is considerable evidence that the 1980s have brought a marked deterioration in living standards for the world's poor. For example, African GDP per capita fell 11% between 1980 and 1985, and in the Middle East the fall was 19.2%.[39] Whereas Third World per capita growth averaged 2.8% p.a. over the 1965–1984 period, from 1980 to 1984 it averaged under 0.9%.[40]

Brown claims that 'Most of the major countries in Africa and all of the major Latin American ones . . . have experienced income declines during this decade.'[41] Langmore concludes that '. . . incomes are now declining for about half the people of the developing world.'[42] A special UNICEF study concluded that malnutrition, low birth weight and numbers of child deaths are now on the increase among the poor in many countries.[43]

It is therefore important not to regard the achievements of the 1950–1970 period as normal. In many ways this was the most remarkable and atypical period in the entire three hundred year history of the world capitalist system, and it would be a serious mistake to base analyses of the prospects for Third World development on the assumption that capital availability, export demand and aid would continue as they did during that period. The achievements of the 1950–1970 period are more sensibly taken as marking the upper limits to realistic expectations regarding the potential of conventional development under extraordinarily favourable conditions.

INCOME DISTRIBUTIONS

In a world with adequate resources to provide for all, and with sufficient productive capacity within all nations, the core problem underlying the plight of most of the world's people is grossly uneven distributions of income, wealth and resources. National income distributions remain extremely uneven, and although some have improved, the overall trend has probably been a deterioration. Figures 4 and 5 present two national income distributions and the changes that have occurred.

When it comes to the world distribution of income we can be more confident that inequality is increasing (see Figure 6). The ratio of rich world GNP per capita to that

Figure 4: India: Income Distributions, 1954 and 1963 (Constant 1954 Rupee)

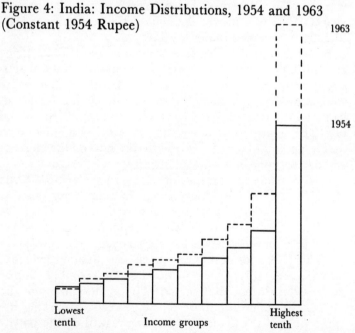

The richest fifth gained 75 times as much as the poorest fifth; real incomes of the poorest tenth fell slightly.

(S. Jain, *The Size Distribution of Income: A Compilation of Data*, Johns Hopkins University Press, 1975, p. 50)

Figure 5: Brazil: Income Distributions, 1970 and 1980

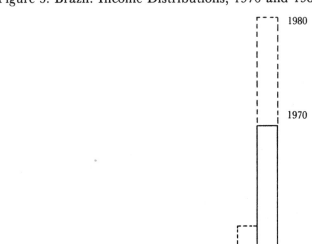

(from D. Denslow and W. Tyler, 'Perspectives on Poverty and Income in Brazil', *World Development* 12, 10, 1019–1028)

of the least developed countries was around 20/1 in 1960 but by 1980 was 46/1.

The immense productive potential of the global economic system is indicated in Figure 6 by the 195% increase in world output over the eight years to 1976 (115% in real or deflated terms). However, the graph shows that very little of the increase in income went to the poorer groups. The richest fifth of the world's people received *67 times* the proportion of the increase received by the poorest fifth! According to World Bank figures the less developed countries received 5.6% of world income in 1978, but only 4.56% in 1984.[44]

The crucial challenge to adherents to the conventional

Figure 6: World: Income Distributions, 1968 and 1976

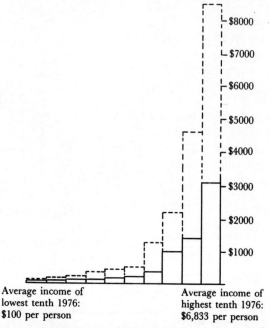

Average income of
lowest tenth 1976:
$100 per person

Average income of
highest tenth 1976:
$6,833 per person

In the period the top fifth gained *67 times* as much of the increase in world income as the bottom fifth.

(from *New Internationalist*, Feb. 1980, p. 5)

approach to development is: what are the reasons for believing that an economic system and an approach to development that yields such distributions of the available wealth will solve the Third World's problems, when those problems are primarily due to receipt of an unsatisfactory share of the world's wealth?

The crucial issue is not simply whether Third World indices are improving or stagnating. (Because Dependency theory claimed stagnation is the key problem, some people have assumed that *any* detectable improvement shows Dependency theory to be wrong and vindicates the conventional approach.) Measured in average GNP terms Third World living standards have improved since 1960, but are we therefore supposed to endorse the global economy and present development strategies when they deliver forty times as large an increase in annual income to the few in the overdeveloped countries as they do to the poorest half of the world's people?

'TRICKLE DOWN' THEORY

Conventional economic theory can largely be summed up by the claim that the best strategy is to promote as much economic growth as possible, even though in the short run the result will be sharper inequality, because in time this will generate much more national wealth and then there will be more to trickle down to all.

Much attention has been given to Kuznetz' hypothesis that as Third World countries develop, inequality *increases* for a period but then begins to decrease.[45] There is hardly any evidence which is directly relevant to the hypothesis, since most of the evidence under discussion has been drawn from a sample of countries at one particular point in time. The important issue is whether *a particular country* undergoing normal capitalist development is likely to experience an increase in inequality, followed by a decrease. There is little evidence on trends over time within particular countries, and what there is does not provide much encouragement to advocates of the Kuznets hypothesis. Even if the hypothesis is correct, this does not mean the conventional approach is acceptable. The question then is whether *the rate* of trickle down is satisfactory, and more importantly whether quite different approaches might be more satisfactory.[46]

Although statements of conventional theory and specific project documents rarely if ever (perhaps never)[47] openly endorse the 'trickle down' mechanism, and even though in the last decade it has been admitted that pursuing growth does not automatically benefit the poor majority, trickle down nevertheless tacitly remains the core premise for conventional discussions of development, in rich as well as

'. . . and then wealth will trickle down to enrich everyone.'

poor countries. The bulk of development advice, planning, aid and theory continues to shy away from any thought of redistributing productive capacity, and to be aimed primarily at stimulating the maximum possible rate of growth of business turnover, on the assumption that this is the surest path to greater wealth for all, including the poor.

Over the past two decades a great deal of evidence has accumulated showing that *very little trickle down ever takes place*. Indeed this may well be the most clearly established proposition to have emerged from three decades of development research. In fact conventional growth strategies often result in the very opposite of trickle down, an effect most tragically evident when the 'modernisation' of agriculture enriches planters, who then increase export crops by terminating the leases of peasant farmers.

By far the most crucial issue for the evaluation of conventional development theory and practice is *the amount or rate* of trickle down. We have seen that, in general, incomes in the poorest half of the world have been rising at about $7 per capita p.a. The question is: how likely is it that this growth and trickle down mechanism will raise the welfare of the world's poor within an acceptable time span? The issue is also one of efficiency: how acceptable is a development strategy which allocates almost all of the world's wealth to the rich few, increasing their per capita wealth by $270 per year, while increasing the income of the poorest half by less than $7 per year? The conventional view implies that those few on a GNP 46 times the poorest half of the world's people should strive to increase their consumption of the world's wealth (they already consume 80% of its resource output) on the grounds that this will continue to add to the income of the poor at a rate of around 3% of what it adds to their own income.

'But hasn't growth and trickle down worked well in the rich countries?' some may ask. 'After all, their working classes have high living standards.' But it was political action, not waiting for trickle down, which delivered these living standards. People organised and fought for minimum wages and the welfare legislation that ensures for them a more reasonable share of national income.

RESOURCE AND ENVIRONMENTAL CONDITIONS

The conventional approach to development requires highly implausible assumptions to be made about the resource and environmental conditions underpinning development. The conditions that could be taken for granted in the long boom, including oil at $1.80 per barrel and negligible environmental protection costs, have disappeared, and these costs are very likely to rise steeply from now on.[48] Some will jump catastrophically as Third World ecosystems, forests and soils deteriorate. In addition there will be more general global ecological impacts such as climate change through greenhouse, ozone and acid rain problems.[49] Brown claims that Africa loses 29 trees for every one planted.[50] In four African countries accounting for one-quarter of the continent's population, mid-1980s crop yields were lower than in the early 1950s, partly due to heavy erosion losses.[51] Many countries are reporting lower grain yields, and world grain yields per hectare have actually fallen after peaking in the early 1970s, despite large increases in fertilizer application.[52]

Development gains evident in financial terms have in part been achieved by selling off ecological capital. Malaysia's timber export earnings represent the loss of forests that will no longer exist in thirty years' time, and whose loss will then impose many other costs, including the cost of alternative sources of food and materials for people presently dependent on the forests, the cost of the soil lost and the increased flooding that will occur without forest cover to hold rainfall, and the cost of the soil nutrients lost when dung has to be burned because there is no fuel wood left. Statements of GNP growth rates and export earnings would have to be discounted significantly for these effects before a real picture of the health of these economies could be assessed.

WHAT ABOUT THE NEWLY INDUSTRIALISING COUNTRIES?

Conventional development thinking has recently placed considerable emphasis on the export-led strategy as the path whereby several Third World nations are demonstrably developing at a rapid pace. This phenomenon has been taken by some as refuting Dependency theory, which claims that capitalist development led by rich countries results in stagnation for the Third World.

This strategy has certainly enabled the Newly Industrialising Countries to achieve remarkable economic growth in recent years, notably Taiwan, South Korea, Hong Kong and Singapore. There is, however, little reason to regard these as models which the rest of the Third World can follow.[53] Two are cities rather than countries, having no huge impoverished rural peasantry, so they are unlikely to provide clues for solving the main Third World problems. The success, and especially the levels of equity, evident in the other two are in part due to the radical land redistributions imposed by external forces around the time of World War II, a phenomenon distinctly unlikely to result from opting for export-oriented industrialisation.

More significantly, all these NICs have prospered by winning the tight competition to export manufactured goods to the quite limited markets of the rich countries. There is only room for a very small number of countries to succeed in that arena. The four countries listed above total a mere 2% of the Third World's population. Some authors, notably Bill Warren,[54] have taken the fact that these very few countries are developing to mean that all are or can. Pilkington clearly points out this mistake.[55]

Even the most successful Third World exporters have run into serious difficulties in the 1980s in the face of rising trade barriers erected by the rich countries. Advocates of the export-oriented approach to development fail to deal with the fact that it could only succeed if there were vast untapped markets in the developed countries, thus permitting continual expansion of Third World manufactured exports.

In reality, however, there is an immense and chronic trade problem. Export markets are glutted, protection is rampant, commodity prices are low, billions are spent to store unsaleable produce, and world trade has virtually stagnated since 1980. By the early 1980s it had become clear that '. . . the favourable international conditions which allowed the Newly Industrialising Country strategy to achieve such success for a period are now disappearing'.[56]

Nor can the development of these countries be regarded as self-sustaining, since they are highly dependent on external conditions, resources and capital. To a considerable extent their growth has been due to development of the sector in which transnational corporations use cheap Third World labour to assemble goods for export.[57] Their development can therefore be in part attributed to those changes in the technology of transport and communications, in wage differentials between rich and poor countries, and global financial systems (including the increased ease of Third World borrowing for infrastructure development), whereby it became favourable for transnational corporations to relocate much of their manufacturing in the Third World. While '. . . multinational corporations may be developing, the people living in the Newly Industrialising Countries are not.'[58]

In addition, the development that has occurred in the Newly Industrialising Countries is far from satisfactory development.[59] It has been accomplished by considerable repression of labour and restrictions on human rights.[60] It is not surprising that South Korea has been able to beat others in the competition for export sales when the average working week in 1987 was 53 hours and there were no free trade unions. Claims about South Korea's economic success must also be seen in relation to its huge debt – $48 billion in 1987 – and violent riots and other expressions of dissent which have been countered with state repression. Taiwan's achievements must be evaluated in relation to the existence of a 38 year period of martial rule which ended only in 1987. These extreme government powers and repressive labour conditions have been important contributors to the lower production costs and the competitive advantage of these two countries.

One thing the NIC phenomenon does seem to show clearly is that state intervention and planning, not free enterprise, is the key to success! Although proclaimed as glowing examples of the free enterprise way, the most successful NICs, especially Taiwan and South Korea, have achieved their success through extensive government initiative and support. Japan's situation is similar. Industries have been protected, advised and guided by state bureaucracies, and given all sorts of assistance in order to ensure their competitiveness on the world stage.

CONCLUSIONS ON THE CONVENTIONAL APPROACH TO DEVELOPMENT

Table 6 summarises positions explicitly stated in approximately a hundred analyses in books and articles I have encountered in recent years, dealing with the record of development achievement since 1970. A few of these comments are included in the accompanying box. Almost all summary comments stated that at best negligible gains had been made for large numbers of Third World people, or for Third World people in general. All comments reviewed on the post-1980 period estimated that absolute living standards had in general fallen, and for large numbers had undergone marked falls. No direct attempts to explain that the conventional strategy is producing satisfactory Third World development were encountered. This literature both criticises the practical achievements of the conventional approach, and rejects conventional development theory. Among academic students of development this theory now encounters widespread criticism and rejection; it is annoying that this is not paralleled by opinion at the level of the general public, nor at the level of governmental agencies.

This table is not based on a statistically random sample, though I would be surprised if it is significantly misleading. My main contention is that critical conclusions are overwhelmingly dominant and that endorsements of the

Table 6: Survey of conclusions on development
achievements

| Conclusion | Number of books or articles Period | | |
	1980s	1975–1980	Not specified
Little or no increase in living standards within the Third World	20	22	7
Falls in real living standards within specified countries	12	10	3
Falls in real living standards in many Third World countries or for large groups within the Third World	12	9	2
Statements claiming significant, marked or satisfactory (or similar terms) progress in real Third World living standards	0	0	possibly 3

Each of the items surveyed appears in only one cell

The relevant quotations have been compiled in Trainer 1986b

conventional theory and practice, let alone arguments or
explanations as to how it is likely to solve the problems,
are almost non-existent.[61]

To summarise the discussion, there is now a very weighty
case against conventional development theory and practice.
Few if any explicit defences ever appear in the development
literature. It is condemned directly or indirectly by a vast
amount of literature and evidence that has accumulated
over the last two decades. It is most unlikely that even if
the conditions of the long boom were to continue this
approach would ever solve the Third World's major problems. If it could eventually do so it would have to be
regarded as an extremely slow, wasteful, inefficient and
unjust strategy, since for every extra crumb it provides to

the needy it delivers loaves to the already rich. Yet it continues to be the dominant, taken-for-granted frame.

The most disturbing point is to do with options forgone. Most poor countries have quite sufficient land, capital and other productive capacity to provide low but adequate living standards for all their people, and the remainder could fairly easily attain that situation in a short time – if the available resources were more evenly distributed, and if the available productive capacity were not largely devoted to the production of things other than those which most people need.

Comments on the Development Record

'Development of the type experienced by the majority of Third World countries in the last quarter century has meant, for very large numbers of people, increased impoverishment. This is the conclusion which has emerged from a series of empirical studies of trends in levels of living in the rural areas of Asia. In most of the countries we have studied, the incomes of the very poor have been falling absolutely or the proportion of the rural population living below a designated "poverty line" has been increasing, or both. Similar things almost certainly have been happening elsewhere, in Africa and parts of Latin America, for the mechanisms which generate poverty in Asia are present in greater or lesser degree in much of the rest of the underdeveloped world'.

'In almost every case a significant proportion of low-income households experienced an absolute decline in their real income, particularly since the early 1960s'.

> K. Griffin and A. R. Kahn, 'Poverty in the Third World: Ugly facts and fancy models', Chapt. 18 in H. Alavi and T. Shanin, Eds., *Introduction to the Sociology of Developing Societies*, 1982.

'Many Third World countries that had experienced relatively high rates of economic growth by historical standards in the 1960s began to realize that such growth had brought little in the way of significant benefits to their poor. For those hundreds of millions of people in Africa, Asia, and Latin America, levels of living seemed to stagnate and in some countries, even to decline in real terms. Rates of rural and urban unemployment and underemployment were on the rise. The distribution of incomes seemed to become less equitable with each passing year. Many people felt that rapid economic growth had failed to eliminate or even reduce widespread absolute poverty, which remained a fact of economic life in all Third World nations'. p. 138

'The magnitude and extent of world poverty has probably worsened over the past two decades'. p. 290

'In the period 1960–1982 there has been little improvement in the per capita incomes of the poorest Third World people'. pp. 30, 85.

M. P. Todaro, *Economic Development in the Third World*, 1985.

'The development strategy pursued by the less developed countries over the past three decades has emphasised urban industrialisation. It has relied upon exports to the developed world to finance this process. This strategy has been broadly unsuccessful ... the strategy has failed to improve markedly the welfare of the general population in most LDCs ... It has failed because it is not appropriate to the needs and resources of most of the developing nations'.

W. Murdoch, *The Poverty of Nations*, Baltimore, Johns Hopkins University Press, 1980, p. 202

'More than any other single fact of the world development situation in the 1970s it is the failure of growth to eliminate poverty that is responsible for the major re-thinking of development goals and strategies that is now in progress across the world'.

H. Brookfield, 'Urban bias, rural bias . . .', in J. W. Land, *Towards a New Strategy for Development*, 1979, p. 98.

'It is now being generally recognised that the conventional development strategy is not a solution to the problem of development in the developing countries.' 'The conventional development strategy is *not* a solution to the problems of international inequality. It is a cause of . . .' those problems.

R. K. Diwan and D. Livingston, *Alternative Development Strategies and Appropriate Technology*, Pergamon, N.Y. 1979.

'Recent studies in a host of countries – including Bangladesh, Indonesia, Malaysia, Pakistan, the Philippines, Thailand and parts of India – indicate that the absolute incomes of some groups have declined over the past two decades, often in the face of considerable growth in gross national product and agricultural output'.

E. Eckholm, *The Disposessed of the Earth*, Worldwatch Paper 30, June 1979, p. 9.

'The failure of rather substantial growth of output in the developing countries to reduce poverty has been widely recognised'.

N. L. Hicks, 'Growth vs Basic Needs: Is there a Trade Off?', *World Development*, 7, 1979, pp. 985–994.

'The key observation is this. In the last thirty years, almost all the hundred-odd LDCs have enjoyed growth and even "development" at unprecedented rates. Yet – with a few exceptions, such as China, Malaysia and Taiwan – the proportion of their populations below a fixed acceptable minimum standard of feeding, housing, clothing, and freedom from chronic illness has not fallen much'.

M. Lipton, *Why The Poor Stay Poor*, 1977, p. 27.

'After three decades (of development effort) there is little doubt that inequality of wealth and income, both internationally and domestically has increased and is still increasing . . . It is undeniable that the poorest, especially in the poorest countries, have suffered an absolute decline in their standard of living'.

T. Balough, 'Failures in the strategy against poverty,' *World Development*, 1978, 6,1, p. 11.

CHAPTER 4

Underdevelopment: Its Essential Nature and Causes

Although there is now a voluminous literature arguing that Third World development is unsatisfactory, it is remarkable that we still do not have anything like a commonly accepted, clear and simple account of what is wrong about development and why. The theory tends to be complicated and difficult to master, and is often stated and discussed in obscure technical language. There are several confused debates raging within and between the various schools of thought. These are sometimes to do with essentials, but often they concern secondary issues. Anyone coming into the arena for the first time would have to read and reread for many months before being able to form even a general impression of what it all means.

It is especially disappointing that teachers, aid agency personnel and journalists do not have access to a fairly standard critique of the core issues, a clear introduction to the nature and causes of underdevelopment, the injustice of the global economy, the relations between rich and poor countries, and what might constitute a satisfactory approach to development.

Consequently, while development educators usually make clear that the current state of development is not satisfactory they find it hard to say much that is at all convincing when it comes to explaining what is wrong, why, and what the best remedies might be.

Most unfortunately, critical analyses often lead only to recommendations and policies which might merely reform the existing global system, when it must be strongly argued that no version of that system can facilitate satisfactory development.

This chapter presents a framework which makes possible a clear, simple and plausible account of what is happening and what is wrong, and which gives development educators a powerful line of argument. One of the main virtues of this framework is that it facilitates evaluation. It gives us a clear guide for moralising, for condemning what is wrong, and for arguing that conventional approaches are disastrously mistaken and that radically different approaches must be endorsed. But first it is necessary to detail the conventional view.

THE CONVENTIONAL, MODERNISATION OR GROWTH VIEW OF DEVELOPMENT

What follows is a brief summary of the view of development which is still generally accepted, especially by government and official development agencies; and, sad to say, by most high school text books and university departments of economics.[62]

1. '**Development is basically about economic growth**. It is about increasing the amount of business turnover, or production for sale, including the amount of investment and trade: 'Just get the economy going and the increase in productive capacity and wealth will automatically solve all other problems, at least faster and better than any other strategy can.'

Since the early 1970s, apologists for the conventional approach have been forced to admit that sheer growth is far from sufficient, and that attention also has to be given to equity and basic needs. But these remain minor considerations, reluctantly tacked on. Sheer increase in the amount of economic activity is still thought to be the essence of development.

It does not take much thought to realise that development must be conceived in terms of improving a society as a whole, and enhancing the welfare or quality of life of all. Consequently, development of the political system, of technology, of social arrangements, of ecosystems, and of the whole geography and culture of the society should be on the agenda. Yet conventional discussions of development proceed as if there were no need to consider anything but the growth of economic activity.

Conventional theory is almost entirely about totally *indiscriminate* economic development. The whole point is to increase the overall level of economic activity, or the total dollar value of producing and consuming, ignoring questions about the appropriateness of what is being produced or developed, about what most needs developing, what developments would be best for people, and what would increase the quality of life. The possibility that some particular economic developments might harm the welfare of some or all people is often regarded as insignificant. The fact that an indiscriminate growth strategy results in vast production of non-necessities and neglects essentials is ignored.

2. '**The causes of underdevelopment lie within the Third World**. They lack the necessary conditions; they do not have enough capital; they lack skills and work motivation. Their governments are corrupt. Their geographical conditions are difficult. They lack modern western values and habits.'

3. '**All countries are moving up the same development path**, on which there are preliminary stages that will culminate in "take off" to the sort of rapid and self-sustaining growth that the rich countries have.'

4. '**The main block to development is lack of capital**. They are poor because they can't save much, and because they can't invest and produce much. In other words there is a self-perpetuating "cycle of poverty". Therefore it is

very important for capital to be brought into the Third World, in the form of foreign investment and aid.'

5. '**The best way to get development going is to assist the few with capital and entrepreneurial talent to invest**. This will generate more factories, jobs and goods, and eventually more wealth for all. It is important not to redistribute the existing wealth in an effort to give the poor a fairer share immediately. In fact it is important to help the already rich few to become much richer, because getting them to invest is the most effective way to generate economic growth.'

6. '**Very uneven development is acceptable**.' The rich few typically become far richer. Good jobs are created for a small number of middle class and urban workers. Development focuses on the small number of people who are capable of buying things. The export sector of the economy tends to grow rapidly. Cities boom, but the rural areas and most people in the country experience little or no immediate benefit as development gets underway. In fact conventional theorists accept that the process typically increases inequality, and can reduce the absolute living standards of many.

7. '**Development must be initiated and led by elites**, by the few who have capital: the experts and the government. They have the wisdom and the technology. The mass of ignorant peasants cannot be expected to have any worthwhile input into policy decisions.'

8. '**Big infrastructure development is vital** – the dams and power grids, the roads and airports that will do most to facilitate the general increase in production, transport and sales.'

9. '**The global economy is basically acceptable**. It is best to have freedom of enterprise and the profit motive operating within a market system. This maximises output and efficiency.'

10. '**The rich nations are eager to facilitate development**. They are not thwarting development, let alone exploiting poor countries.'

11. '**A highly integrated world economy is desirable**. It is best if there is much trade, foreign investment and lending, and if there is freedom of access for firms to operate in other nations. Interdependence maximises the ability to specialise and gain comparative advantage. It is not desirable that countries attempt to minimise involvement in the global economy and strive for self-sufficiency.'

12. '**There will be trickle down**.' This is the crucially important premise in conventional development theory. The entire approach is based on the idea that by enabling the rich to become much richer as quickly as possible through investing in whatever promises to maximise their incomes, '. . . national wealth will grow at the fastest possible rate – and then there will be more to trickle down to all. There will then be more goods available and more poor people will be able to get jobs as more factories open up. The new wages will generate more demand for more goods and more factories.'

13. '**They must modernise**.' Many Third World countries have lifestyles and traditions which do not facilitate efficient production in modern Western factories and offices. They must become punctual, hard working, competitive, achievement-oriented, disciplined, and concerned to raise their material living standards. The industrialised, commercialised Western consumer way of life is the model to which the Third World should aspire.

14. '**It is physically possible for the Third World to rise to the material lifestyles which the rich countries have**: there are enough energy, mineral and environmental resources to make this possible.' Chapter 6 will show that this is one of the most unacceptable premises of conventional theory.

THE KEY: MARKET FORCES PRODUCE INAPPROPRIATE DEVELOPMENT

Having dispensed with the preliminaries, it is time to plunge into the core issue. How can we best represent what is wrong with this model of development, and why?

The central argument in this book is that by far the best way to make sense of development is to focus on the way in which market forces work, on what happens when we allow access to scarce goods to be determined by those who can pay the most, and when we allow decisions about what will be invested in or developed to be settled by what is most profitable for those doing the investing.

There is now a global market system which incorporates many national and local markets, right down to the neighbourhood and household level. Fundamental to an understanding of what is wrong about Third World development is the fact that *markets have a powerful, indeed typically overwhelming, tendency to make the wrong development and distribution decisions*. This assertion clashes head on with the conventional economist's conviction that the market is the most desirable mechanism for making economic decisions. It also clashes with marxist theory, because marxists regard market relations as merely superficial aspects of our economy. They insist that the essential nature of capitalism and its faults must be understood in terms of the 'relations of production', rather than the capitalist market mechanisms of exchange and consumption (see Chapter 8).

The three major ways in which global market forces condemn most of the Third World to inappropriate development are as follows:

1. **Market forces allow the relatively rich few to take most or all of the available resources**. The one quarter of the world's people who live in the developed countries, East and West, consume approximately four-fifths of the resources produced for sale. Their per capita resource consumption is approximately seventeen times that of the poorest half of the world's people. The USA uses 440 times

as much of the world's energy as Bangladesh, and its per capita consumption is 600 times that of Ethiopia.

How the Market Distributes Grain

- The number of people without   730 million
  sufficient food
- The amount of food that would   approx. 40
  eliminate world hunger, p.a.   million tonnes[63]
- The amount of food aid, p.a.   approx. 10
                                     million tonnes
- *The amount of grain fed to animals*   *over 540*
  in the rich countries, p.a.   *million tonnes*

Why? Far more profitable to produce feedlot beef, pork and chicken than to feed hungry people.

While at least a hundred million Cokes are consumed daily, according to UNICEF more than 40,000 children die every day because they are deprived of resources. Lack of access to clean water probably takes ten million lives each year. Hundreds of millions are in need of fuel to sterilise dangerous drinking water but must do without it, while people in rich countries can drive ski boats, because we can offer more money for the fuel.

These grotesque maldistributions of the world's resource wealth come about primarily because rich countries can outbid poor countries. What might have been the development history of Bangladesh or Tanzania had world resource wealth been distributed equally or according to need, rather than according to market forces?

How The Market (Mal) distributes Things

'The market playing freely will always feed the rich'.
    Director-general of FAO, quoted in *New Internationalist*, Jan. 1980, p. 13.

'A market system . . . makes the strong stronger and the weak weaker. . . . Markets as masters of society enrich the rich and pauperize the poor.

Mahbub Ul Haq, *The Poverty Curtain,* 1976, p. xii.

'. . . the concept of market demand mocks poverty or plainly ignores it as the poor have very little purchasing power. . . . The world market system has continuously operated to increase the power and the wealth of the rich and maintain the relative deprivation of the poor.'

Mahbub Ul Haq, in *New Internationalist,* 1975, p. 23.

'. . . capitalism . . . works in such a way that resources are shifted to those who can best pay for them, the rich, and not to those who need them most, the poor.'

G. Lacey, *Enabling All To Survive,* 1976, p. 6.

A MARKET ECONOMY IS AN INGENIOUS DEVICE FOR ENSURING THAT WHEN THINGS BECOME SCARCE ONLY THE RICH CAN GET THEM.

'Sure, I could sell it to you for $1 and make a small profit –
but I can sell it to him for $34!!'

2. **Market forces have predominantly developed the wrong industries in the Third World**. A great deal of development has taken place; the trouble is that it has not been development of the most needed industries. It has been mostly the development of industries to provide crops and consumer goods for the small rich local elites or for export to the rich countries.

What most needs developing in a typical Third World country? More cheap housing, clean water supplies, mobile rural health clinics, and simple tools. But the sorts of things mostly being developed are Hilton Hotels, international airports, TV assembly factories and coffee plantations – because investing in these enterprises promises far greater profits.

3. **Much of the Third World's productive capacity has become geared to the demand of the developed countries**. This is most evident in the case of export crops. Over 20 million hectares produce tea, coffee and cocoa for export.[64] In some countries (such as the Philippines) half the best land grows crops to export to the rich countries. These are again direct consequences of allowing the highest bid to determine the uses to which the Third World's productive capacity is put.

Drawing Development Resources into the Wrong Purposes

In the decade to 1973 87% of all credit provided by the Guatemalan government went to finance export production, while only 3% went to rice, corn and beans which local people eat.

> N. Chomsky, *Turning the Tide*, London, Pluto, 1986, p. 40.

In Latin America 90% of fertilizer is used for purposes other than producing basic food for local people.

> W. Murdoch, *The Poverty of Nations*, 1980, p. 162.

The core problem is not the lack of development; it is the <u>inappropriateness</u> of development. The problem is not stagnation; in fact there is far too much development – of the wrong things. Nor is the basic problem loss of surplus. There is quite enough capital in the Third World to establish necessary appropriate industries and infrastructures, those which would enable the poor majority to produce for themselves the things they need for low but reasonable living standards. That capital is presently being used by foreign investors to produce highly inappropriate goods.

There are decisions which the market can make effectively, and we could allow market forces to handle them in a satisfactory economy. If someone thinks it would be a good idea to produce jam in a smaller container than is currently on sale, for example, then the market might be the simplest and most efficient way of determining whether or not that is a good idea. There are millions of decisions to do with adjusting supply and demand that might best be left to market forces. The point of the foregoing argument is that there are very definite limits to the sorts of decision it is sensible to leave to the market. When there is significant inequality in purchasing power it is disastrous to let markets decide what is to be produced and who is to get scarce resources. In a sane and humane world these and many other decisions would be made in a rational and deliberate way through some mechanism whereby society as a whole could consider the issue and plan appropriate distribution and investment policies. (Of course the process ought to be highly participatory and democratic; leaving social planning to state bureaucrats is not the answer.)

I am not claiming that it is only a free and competitive market which determines what happens in development. Corporations, governments and other agencies often have the power to influence or set market conditions or to overrule them altogether. But this is only to say that the richest and most powerful participants in the global economy often have *even more* capacity to take or develop what they want

Look! Development!

than would arise solely from their ability to make the highest bid in a free and competitive market.

There is a large literature making the point that to allow market forces, the profit motive and the maximisation of economic growth to be the overwhelming determinants of development is to guarantee that mostly inappropriate development will result.[65]

RE-EXAMINING CONVENTIONAL THEORY IN TERMS OF MARKET FORCES

We should now reconsider some of the assumptions and claims made by modernisation or growth theory in the light of this examination of the way in which a market system functions, in order to see how readily the mistakes and the undesirable outcomes are explained if we focus on market forces and inappropriateness.

'**Development = growth**.' The fundamental mistake which modernisation theory makes is the assumption that simply encouraging as much economic growth as possible will result in satisfactory development.

The first objection is to the *indiscriminate* nature of a single-minded growth strategy. There is no concern to identify what most needs producing or developing. The goal is simply to increase output of anything that those with capital want to produce. Do we need more bubble gum? A conventional economist is perfectly happy to see more bubble gum produced and sold, because that means more jobs and taxes. His development theory leaves him totally unable to discriminate between such inappropriate production and things that make sense in terms of human need and welfare.

Secondly, as we have seen, where participants in a market system have significantly unequal purchasing power there is a head-on contradiction between what is most profitable and what is most needed. The investments that will generate most GNP and return most profit will be those which produce relatively unnecessary items, or which supply scarce resources to richer groups. If you have money to invest you will not make much profit from investing in cheap basic necessities for impoverished people. So when the development goal is seen to be simply getting as much economic activity as possible going you can be sure that mostly inappropriate things will be developed. Usually the developments most likely to add to the rate of growth of GNP, such as a Volkswagen assembly plant or another coffee plantation, are clearly those most unlikely to improve the lot of the poor majority. Most people need clean water, not Volkswagens. Conversely, the most needed developments in the Third World, such as providing clean water supplies and mobile health clinics, redistributing land, and increasing subsistance crop production, would add little to the GNP, and may even reduce it by taking productive resources out of ventures presently generating high cash earnings, through such measures as the conversion of export plantations to peasant holdings.

It is worth noting that both Marxists and Dependency theorists share this fundamental conception of development being equivalent to indiscriminate economic growth. Their primary concern is the same as that of conventional theorists – to see an increase in the sheer volume of economic activity, business turnover, and producing and consuming. The essential complaint which Dependency theory makes is that normal capitalist growth in the Third World has been blocked. Marxists, on the other hand, believe that the more rapidly capitalism grows the sooner it will self-destruct in revolution. Neither of these theories has much interest in what is being invested in or produced, nor in any conception of appropriate development. They do not focus on questions such as, 'What needs developing here?' or 'Are appropriate things being developed here.'*

---

* Marxists certainly do concern themselves with 'socially useful' production, and would be among the first to agree that Third World development is largely inappropriate, but recent Marxist literature on Third World development gives little or no

The turning point for this conception of development has come with the accumulation of abundant evidence that very little trickle down ever takes place. A sheer growth approach might have made some sense if, despite its gross inefficiency, it did eventually meet the basic needs of the poor majority. Even if the resource and environment future were capable of sustaining an indiscriminate growth approach to development, however, it has been increasingly clear since the 1960s that this results in little more than development in the interests of the rich. It produces the distributions shown in Figures 4, 5 and 6. It does little or nothing for the 40% of the world's people in greatest need. In fact the indiscriminate, sheer-growth conception of development causes immense havoc among the poor. It has stripped them from the land and moved them to urban slums, it has made large numbers poorer and hungrier, and it has destroyed their forests to build dams.

It is therefore essential that attention be shifted from the idea that development equals growth, and focused on the question of what specific things are appropriate to develop. Often the answer is: Very few! It is distressingly obvious that people living in largely self-sufficient ways in unspoiled ecosystems and with rich social and cultural systems need only a few additional basic goods and services, emergency medical care perhaps, or relief from some arduous labour, or somewhat improved gardening techniques, in order to enjoy a high and secure quality of life despite low GNP per capita.

Technically it would be very easy for these appropriate developments to be achieved, through the introduction of a small number of simple devices and systems using local inputs augmented by minimal imports. What is required could often be established in a matter of months. But the conventional development path is totally different. It

___

attention to what might constitute appropriate development, or to promoting it.

obliges them to encourage entrepreneurs to start producing items which local people neither want nor can afford, and to export these to the rich, using up local forests or other resources and yielding low wages to local people, thus enticing or forcing them into plantations and factories and into the cash economy. They then become addicted to Western consumer goods and dependent upon the predatory international economic system, in the hope that after many decades – or even possibly generations – this process, which will gear most of their increasing productive capacity to the benefit of others, will yield sufficient crumbs to enable the people in general to rise to tolerable living standards.

To contemplate many underdeveloped countries, with their rich forests still intact and in need of very little development, from the problem-ridden capitals of the most 'developed' countries, raises profoundly disturbing questions about what constitutes satisfactory development, and what the identification of development with indiscriminate growth has done to many societies which might have otherwise have easily achieved the few developments that make sense for them. Conventional theory never questions the tragic assumption that to develop is to set out on the path that ends up in down-town Los Angeles. It has no other vision than that of a series of stages leading to a modern industrialised-consumer society. Chapter 6 will show that this is neither possible nor desirable. It is of the utmost importance that the many countries needing development of some sort should reject this indiscriminate assumption and focus on the question, 'To what sort of society do we wish to develop; what things should we develop?'

It cannot be overemphasised that growth and the market are the problems. The Third World's plight is essentially a matter of maldistribution and deprivation. Huge numbers are without sufficient food and materials for reasonable lifestyles and, more importantly, without the small amounts of productive capacity that would enable them to produce for themselves most of what they need.

The required land, water and capital exist in adequate and often abundant quantity in most, if not all, poor countries. *It is the normal functioning of the global market economy which delivers the available resources to a few and deprives the majority.* The drive to maximise output, sales and returns on investent *inevitably* leads to the focusing of productive capacity on the already rich. They are the ones most able to make the highest bid in the market and to maximise consumption of increased output; producing luxuries for them is much more likely to increase returns on investment than producing necessities for destitute people. Consequently the extremely uneven distributions in Figures 4, 5 and 6, and their deterioration over time are inevitable outcomes of an economic system and an approach to development which allows the market to determine what is developed and who gets the wealth produced, and of a system which is about maximising the amount of production for sale. The conventional growth and trickle down view always sees the solution to the problems of the poor world as cranking up to even higher rates of economic growth, but <u>this is to accelerate the very mechanism that has caused the problem</u>.

'He says the more he grows the more crumbs we'll get'

Two decades ago none of this was at all clear. It was quite plausible that baking a bigger cake was the wise course of action. The great difference is that now we have extensive evidence about how little wealth trickles down, even under boom conditions. It is now very difficult to escape the conclusion that satisfactory development for the Third World as a whole cannot result from such a mechanism, and that satisfactory development is not possible unless there is radical redistribution from rich to poor, and the adoption of economic strategies which will ensure many outcomes *contrary* to those produced by market forces and the maximisation of growth. It is not that the rich world must charitably redistribute some of its wealth to the poor; it is that the rich world must cease taking such a disproportionate share of the world's wealth.

Another highly undesirable consequence of the conventional view is that nothing but *economic* development matters. Although there is a largely separate literature on political development, the dominant assumption has been that increasing the amount of economic turnover in a society will automatically lead to the satisfactory development of *all* other aspects of that society.

In an ideal society, the economy would be of quite minor importance. We would produce all the required goods and services without much bother, leaving most of our time and energy free to be devoted to maintaining and developing and enjoying our ecological systems, our political systems, our social arrangements, our culture and our personal growth, in artistic, spiritual and other realms. Anyone who insists on thinking about the current development scene in terms of appropriateness must ask whether proposals are likely to promote satisfactory development in these crucial non-economic and typically neglected areas.

To summarise all this in another way, conventional development theory and practice is merely *capitalist* development theory. To conceive of development as indiscriminate economic growth is to opt for the view which most suits the capitalist class, since their fundamental interest is in maximising the amount of investing and selling taking place, and in not having to bother about whether capital really ought to go into things that are appropriate but not very profitable.

The failure of trickle down, and an increasing awareness of environmental and social effects, have made it clear that such a conception of development does not best serve the interests of other classes. Again the evidence on trickle down constitutes the crucial watershed; before that evidence became clear few could doubt that what was best for General Motors was best for everyone. The wider significance of the recent decades of development experience lies in the challenge it sets to the taken-for-granted assumption that indiscriminate growth should also be the supremely important development goal for even the richest countries.

None of this means that existing big-state socialist or communist approaches to development are the answer. Although these typically perform far better than the capitalist approach on a number of important indices to do with basic needs, they also have very serious drawbacks to do with human rights and democratic participation.

'The causes of undervelopment lie within the Third World.' To focus on the way the market system treats participants is to make it clear how relatively unimportant Third World 'deficiencies' are in explaining its poor development record. The internal factors which conventional theorists usually list – lack of expertise, corruption, difficult climates – are certainly part of the explanation, but far more important is the way in which market forces prevent poor countries from getting anything like their fair share of world resources, and ensure that mostly inappropriate things are developed. Again, what might the development record of Tanzania or Bangladesh have been had they had access to an equal share of the world's resources of oil, fertilizer and capital?

'The main block to development is lack of capital.' This claim is easily dismissed. About 85–90% of all the money that foreign investors invest in the Third World is raised within the Third World, usually as loans from Third World banks. This means that there is quite enough capital in the Third World to develop the things required to provide adequate living standards for all. The trouble is of course that almost all the capital is usually in the hands of a very small and very greedy rich class which has no intention of investing it in ventures that would produce what most people need, and less interest in giving people in general any access to it. They prefer to lend to foreign investors, or to speculate, or buy more land, or purchase imported luxuries – or send their capital out to safe foreign banks.

'Very uneven development is acceptable.' This is an inevitable consequence of allowing development to be determined by profit maximisation and market forces. The few with capital will put it into ventures designed to supply those who have the most money to spend, which is to say the rich and the small middle class groups, and the consumers in the developed countries. Hence there is usually rapid growth of the urban and exporting sectors and little or no development in the sectors where the majority of poor people are to be found.

'The global economy is basically acceptable.' Faith in the market typically blinds the conventional economist to the catastrophic and literally murderous effects that market forces generate in the Third World. The lives of millions of children are endangered because gas-guzzling cars and speedboats in the overdeveloped countries can outbid them for the world's scarce petroleum, and they are therefore unable to sterilise contaminated drinking water. Perhaps ten million people die each year because they cannot purchase or grow enough food. It would only take about forty million tonnes of grain p.a. to eliminate hunger from the world, but about fifteen times as much grain as this is fed to animals in the rich countries every year,[66] because it is far more profitable to produce grain for animal feedlots. As has been emphasised before, the Third World problem is basically to do with deprivation and maldistribution of the existing sufficient resources. The global market system is the immediate cause of that maldistribution. The system is massively and grotesquely unjust – it denies reasonable living standards to most people on earth, it condemns at least a billion people to miserable lives, and it is the main link in the chain that causes up to 80,000 avoidable deaths every day.

'The rich nations don't exploit, they facilitate development.' The rich nations certainly do facilitate development – of the wrong things. They promote development of industries in the Third World which will benefit mostly themselves. It is not that rich nations consciously set out to exploit poor nations; it is that they practice and promote an approach to development which works almost entirely in the interests of the rich countries and Third World elites, and which draws Third World productive capacity into producing for these groups when it should be producing what the majority of Third World people need. For the most part this has probably been due to a conscientious but mistaken belief that free enterprise, market forces, the profit motive, indiscriminate economic growth and trickle down would work out best for the majority of Third World people.

'There will be trickle down.' Clearly conventional development is largely development in the interests of the already rich. It can generate rapid increases in productive capacity and wealth, and some Third World countries have sustained remarkable growth rates, but in general very little trickles down. If the goal is to develop the things that most need developing and to meet the needs of the people, then the process has to be regarded as extraordinarily inefficient and wasteful. For each extra loaf of national wealth or productive capacity it generates, only a few crumbs go to those who most need more wealth and productive capacity, while almost all of the benefit goes to the already rich.

The same absurd paradox is evident in the richest countries. The dominant development ideology insists that it would be a mistake to redistribute more wealth from rich to poor, and that the best solution to problems of poverty and other urgent social needs is to enable the rich to invest more profitably so that there will be more jobs, more taxes paid, and more wealth for all. Yet this approach delivers something like twenty times as much of any increase in wealth to the already rich as it does to the poor.

Consider for example the fact that in rich countries we urgently need more housing for low income families. We do not need more speedboat factories. But we allow those with capital to invest in speedboat production and any other non-necessities they might choose. For each pound invested the government collects perhaps 15p in company tax and taxes on wages, of which perhaps 5p is spent on welfare in general, and maybe a fraction of a penny spent on housing. While what we urgently need is more housing, this way we end up with less than a penny more to spend on housing for each pound's worth of new speedboats, when we could have made sure that the whole pound went into housing! How inefficient would a bureaucratically planned economy have to be before it yielded such a small proportion of what was really needed for each pound invested? Yet our free enterprise way is supposed to be the most efficient way. It can of course be quite efficient at doing things like producing speedboats, **but it is appallingly inefficient and morally disgusting when it comes to applying existing productive capacity to meeting existing human needs**. Obviously a system which allows those few who own all the capital to put it into producing what will maximise their profits works primarily in their interests. They get most from investing in items like speedboats – and then they buy the speedboats!

Development – Who Benefits?

'In Honduras, for example, one in eight infants dies before age two and of those who survive to age five, three-quarters are undernourished. The problem is not that food production is insufficient; in 1980, Oxfam reports, "the harvest of bananas was three times greater than the harvest of corn, rice, sorghum and beans combined" while Honduras has become a net importer of all of these staple foods. Coffee, beef, cotton, fruit and palm oil are major export crops, enriching US agribusiness and the tiny elite of Hondurans who are "junior partners with US-based agribusiness companies." Beef production more than doubled since 1960 while per capita consumption of beef declined and exports increased over 500% for hamburgers, hot dogs and pet foods in the US. Forests are being destroyed for cattle ranching, with the assistance of USAID grants funding the expansion of beef production for export. In one typical region, 68% of loans from US government and private sources went to cattle ranchers, 22% to cotton growers, 5% to corn farmers.'

N. Chomsky, *Turning the Tide*, London, Pluto, 1986, p. 39.

If the foregoing analysis is valid, the inescapable conclusion is that satisfactory development is inconceivable without radical change and redistribution. It will not result from continued pursuit of growth, enrichment of the already rich, and trickle down. But the need is not so much for redistribution of *existing wealth* from rich to poor; what is most needed is a redistribution of the *existing productive capacity*, especially the land, so that people can produce for themselves the things that they need for modest but adequate living standards.

CHAPTER 5

Exploring Inappropriate Development

This chapter extends the analysis of development in terms of market forces and inappropriate development. It deals mainly with foreign investment, trade, aid, and food and agriculture.

FOREIGN INVESTMENT

Modernisation or growth theory takes it for granted that foreign investment has a crucial contribution to make to Third World development. The underlying assumption is that Third World countries are poor and therefore lack capital, so it is desirable that foreign investors should bring capital in from rich countries and set up firms long before the poor countries could do so on their own.

We have seen that the major premise here is quite mistaken: the Third World has quite enough capital to develop what is needed, and foreign investors raise about 85% of their funds in the Third World. But this is just the beginning of the story. There are several other disturbing points to be made about foreign investment.

Firstly, foreign investment results in large profit flows back to the rich countries. There is considerable evidence that the total amount being sent home each year is one to three times as much as the amount of new investment capital flowing into the Third World.[67] This means that far from being a source of capital flow to the Third World, foreign investment is a mechanism which has the net effect of draining considerable sums of capital out of the Third World.

Foreign Investment Drains Capital Out

'As various Economic Commission for Latin America reports have shown, the haemorrhage of profits from direct US investments in Latin America has been 5 times greater in recent years than the infusion of new investments.'

E. Galeano, *The Open Veins of Latin America*, 1973, p. 228.

'For each dollar American corporations invested in the Philippines between 1946 and 1976, $3.58 profit was made and $2 of this was repatriated to the U.S.'

W. Bellow, *Development Debacle*, 1982, p. 18.

'In the period 1966–1978, U.S. multinational corporations exported $11 billion to invest in underdeveloped countries, but the return flow to the U.S. on this investment was a fabulous $56 billion. In addition there were profits reinvested in the country of origin.'

The editors, 'U.S. foreign policy in the 1980s', *Monthly Review*, April, 1980.

Harrington refers to a U.N. estimate that in 1970 $2.6 billion flowed into the Third World as foreign investment, but $7.9 billion flowed out as profits on investment.

M. Harrington, *The Vast Majority*, 1977, p. 142.

But, conventional theorists argue, what about the development and the export earnings stimulated by the capital while it is there? The investment does generate plant, jobs and economic activity. However, recent evidence indicates that, contrary to what one would imagine, in the long run foreign investment tends to *slow* economic growth down rather than to promote it. The detailed statistical studies of Bornschier and others[68] show that in the short term foreign investment does result in a boost to economic activity, but in the long term the more foreign investment a Third World country has received, the slower its growth rate is. This seems to be due in part to the tendency for corporations to ease up and sit on their newly conquered domains.

What about all the jobs that foreign investment creates? Relative to the Third World's unemployment problem, foreign investment creates only a miniscule number of jobs. The total at present might be fifteen million, or even much lower.[69] In addition, the coming of the transnational corporation often bankrupts local firms or throws many local craftsmen out of work. Bornschier and Chase-Dunn claim that transnational corporations 'intensify structural unemployment'.[70] Herman says: 'The opening up of Argentina, Brazil and Chile to a heavy influx of foreign capital decimated small and medium sized local manufacturing and other business.'[71]

World unemployment is now of the order of three hundred million, and Third World population will probably rise from 3.5 billion to 8 or 9 billion in the next two or three generations. One of the most forceful arguments against the conventional approach to development is that it has no chance of providing jobs and incomes to all who need them, especially when technical advance is rapidly reducing the need for labour. This is one of the many issues pointing to the need for solutions based on labour-intensive, largely cooperative, village-based development in regionally self-sufficient economies.

What about the transfer of technology? Do not transnational corporations bring in modern procedures? They do, but in many cases there is little scope for these to be used outside the company's high-tech subsidiary.

What about the other economic 'linkages' – will not the

new factory stimulate the local industries that can supply its inputs? To some extent this happens, but often a very high proportion of the corporation's inputs are imported. Often a subsidiary simply imports components from another subsidiary of the same company and assembles them. After all, the main point of locating in the Third World is to use cheap local labour.

But, you may say, the corporations do pay higher wages than local firms. In general this is so, although these wages are usually still very low compared with payment for the same work in the rich countries; perhaps only one-fifth or even one-tenth of the amount.

What about the taxes the companies pay? Surely foreign investment contributes to government revenue and therefore facilitates whatever development the government initiates. Third World countries stampeded into 'export-led' development strategies and competed with each other to attract corporations, setting very advantageous conditions. Among these were low taxes. Often a corporation is allowed to operate without paying any tax at all for a period of five to ten years; in some cases even up to twenty years. Some corporations operate enthusiastically for five or ten years and then, surprise surprise, find that it is in their interests to relocate somewhere else. But there is a much more serious problem deriving from the tax holiday provision: transfer pricing.

Because transnational corporations now have so many subsidiaries all around the world, a high proportion of world exports, probably more than half,[72] take the form of exports from a subsidiary of a corporation in one country to another subsidiary of the same corporation in another country. Your fridge or car or radio has probably done much more travelling than you will ever do. Its components might have been made in many different countries and shipped from one country to another for different processes to be performed. Many of the countries where subsidiaries have been set up to take advantage of cheap labour impose very low taxes, so if the corporation can organise its books so as to appear to make most of its profits in its subsidiaries in those countries, it will minimise its overall tax payment. This is easily done by putting appropriate invoices on goods as they move from one subsidiary to another. When goods flow into a country imposing high taxes, the corporation can charge inflated prices to its subsidiary in that country, and when they flow out to another subsidiary of the corporation low prices can be charged to that subsidiary. As a result the subsidiary in the high tax country does not make much profit. Similarly, subsidiaries in countries where taxes are low can have low prices put on the goods they receive from other subsidiaries, and can put high prices on the goods they export to other subsidiaries, so that the subsidiaries in the low tax countries end up making high profits. Note that another condition which Third World countries often use to attract corporations is granting them freedom to repatriate their profits, allowing them to send profits back to head office rather than obliging them to be reinvested.

This transfer pricing mechanism provides transnational corporations with considerable scope for avoiding taxes. Remember that in rich countries they are supposed to pay about half their profits in taxes, so every pound smuggled out means 50p less tax and 50p more real profit.

It is quite difficult for taxation authorities to find out exactly what is going on, but some of the cases that have been uncovered reveal tax avoidance on a gigantic scale. The most celebrated case concerned importation of drugs into Colombia. Taxation officials found that while the rate of profit declared to them was 6.7%, the real rate disguised by transfer pricing was 137%. Some items were artificially priced around 63 times their normal price in order to reduce apparent profits in Colombia. Altogether around $10 million in tax was avoided.[73]

In another case the UK tax authorities found that Hoffman La Roche had declared a $4 million profit on Valium and Librium sales, but had actually transferred another $21 million to their Geneva head office by setting artificially high charges on their imports of these drugs to their UK subsidiaries. One ingredient costing about £20 per kilo on the international market was being priced at £922 per kilo. The UK Monopolies Commission calculated that the real profit rate for sales of the two drugs was 55% and 60%.[74]

Harrison[75] estimates that whereas in the late 1970s declared profits on foreign investment in the Third World amounted to around $7.5 billion p.a., profits sent home via transfer arrangements might total $20–90 billion every year. Compare this with official development aid in 1977 totalling $17 billion. Since the scope of corporation activities is increasing, it is not surprising that many are paying less tax as the years go by, and that in general the share of tax paid by corporations is falling.

These indictments against foreign investment might seem to constitute a fairly weighty case, but the worst is yet to come. The most serious criticism of foreign investment in the Third World is simply that if left free of control, as it usually is, **it never goes into what most needs doing**. It will always go into those ventures which promise the most profit, and these will always be developments intended to supply relatively expensive goods and luxuries to the local middle class and rich, or to the consumers in the rich countries. Foreign investors *never* go into the Third World to invest in clean drinking water supply, mobile health clinics, or cheap and staple foods for impoverished people – because you do not make much profit from these sorts of ventures. Note that you could make a *small profit* from producing much-needed items like this. Oil, for example, could be sold to very poor villagers at around 60c a barrel, plus shipping costs, because it still costs only 20–50c a barrel to produce oil.[76] Yet in our economy things like this are just not done. You sell at the price likely to maximise your profits, and you invest in those developments likely to maximise your profits.

Foreign Investment Ignores Need

'There is more money to be made from air-conditioners than tube wells, from television than staple foodstuffs. And even when multinationals do venture into agriculture it's more likely to be in producing flowers or pet foods for markets in rich countries than in feeding the people of the developing country itself.'
New Internationalist, Oct., 1978, p. 23.

'. . . any Western multinational company contemplating an investment in the poor nations will easily realise that the greatest purchasing power, and the most likely potential for greatest profit, is to be found among the richest 5 or 20 per cent of the population . . . we can safely assume that the multinational companies only very rarely make investments that are intended to supply the poorest groups of the poor societies with the bare essentials of life. It would, in a free market economy simply be bad business.'
G. Adler-Karlsson, *The Political Economy of East-West-South Cooperation*, 1977, p. 139.

'. . . there seems little doubt that the transnational corporations in general are an obstacle to real development. The basic problem is that the goals of the transnational corporation do not conform to the requirements of real development, particularly the needs of the poor majority in the LDCs.' The corporations '. . . produce generally inessential and inappropriate goods in relation to LDC needs.'
W. Murdoch, *The Poverty of Nations*, Baltimore, Johns Hopkins University Press, 1980, p. 257.

Foreign investment could play a morally acceptable role

if it were carefully controlled by the governments of the Third World countries, and confined to projects that would provide basic necessities. There are many instances of this, such as where governments arrange for foreign contractors to build appropriate infrastructures. However, this runs against the spirit of free enterprise; it is seen as bureaucratic, 'socialistic' state planning, contrary to the all-important market forces.

Hence we come again to the gigantic and deadly paradox: profit is at best indifferent to need, and often contrary to it. Foreign investment will always go into whatever promises to maximise profit, and will totally ignore what most Third World people need to have developed. What is even worse, foreign investment often destroys the existing meagre capacity of local people to provide for themselves, for example where the import of plastic shoes puts local shoemakers out of business.

This issue reveals that the essential things that are wrong about development are not primarily due to evil intent or to any conscious desire to loot or deprive. Indeed the worst effects are motivated by the conscientious belief that development is being furthered. A glance at the way foreign investment works out shows that the main fault lies in the global economic system. A system driven by profit, growth, competition and market forces will inevitably ignore and deprive the poor, and squander resources on the rich.

A common argument encountered in discussions of foreign investment and imperialism is that profit on foreign investment represents such a small proportion of Third World GNP and of total corporation profits that foreign investment cannot possibly be stifling development by depleting the capital available for investment. A similar argument is that the sum is such a minute fraction of the GNP of rich countries that foreign investment and imperialism cannot be necessary for the survival of capitalism as Lenin claimed and many Marxists believe. It is unfortunate that due to the lack of a clear and simple radical account of development, people often appeal to

Which one will he invest in?

some version of Lenin's argument. The argument might in fact be valid, but to say the least it is a difficult argument to sustain and it is far from settled. Fortunately the issue can be avoided, again by focusing on the concept of appropriateness.

The basic criticism concerning imperialism is not that foreign investment depletes available development capital, but that it is part of the process whereby the Third World's development resources are channelled into inappropriate purposes. Even when the sums involved are only small proportions of GNP, the important points are, firstly, that even these amounts could do wonders if devoted to appropriate purposes (since appropriate technologies are not capital-intensive) and, more importantly, where the strategy emphasises growth of corporate and other business activity, the rest of the economy becomes geared to, or neglected in favour of, this sector. Thus even if the business sector is quite small and siphons out a negligible proportion of GNP, *it pre-empts and thwarts* other development initiatives. For example, where the important goal is taken to be making mines function more effectively, it is unlikely that there will be any interest on the part of development officials in making land available for unemployed and low paid miners to grow their own food.

TRADE

Conventional development theory assumes that it is important for Third World countries to engage enthusiastically in international trade. For a long time the dominant view has urged them to specialise in the export of the few agricultural or mineral products they could best produce, and in which they had a 'comparative advantage' in relation to other countries. To some extent this theory makes sense, but it has led most poor countries to derive nearly all their export earnings from a very small number of commodity exports, sometimes only one or two. Even in the 1980s nearly half the Third World nations received more than 50% of their export earnings from one primary product.[77] This leaves a country highly vulnerable to changes in the fickle global economy. A sudden price fall can devastate national accounts and planning, and countries must compete against each other, offering lower prices for their main crop because the buyers are a few giant monopolised corporations.

Adhering to the comparative advantage strategy has contributed to the dependence many poor countries now suffer. Even a country like Cuba which left the free enterprise sphere decades ago has not been able to break its dependence on sugar exports.

The export-led development strategy

In the late 1960s the emphasis turned to the exporting of manufactured goods as the key to development. Many countries have gone to great lengths to set up or attract industries that will manufacture goods to supply to the rich countries. A number of countries have enjoyed remarkable success in this export strategy, and have been labelled the Newly Industrialising Countries (NICs).

In the 1970s it was often argued that the rapid growth of countries like South Korea and Taiwan through export-led development strategies constituted a model which Third World countries could follow to prosperity. This is a quite unrealistic hope, mainly because there is no chance of many countries prospering by exporting manufactured goods to the rich countries. In Chapter 3 it was explained how those markets are now glutted, with protective barriers everywhere. In the 1980s even the most successful Newly Industrialising Countries have run into serious problems through their inability to maintain their export performance.

Free-trade zones

The Newly Industrialising Countries have led the way in setting up many Free Trade Zones, special sites on which transnational corporations have been invited to establish manufacturing plants. Third World governments have invested considerable sums in providing roads, water, power and other infrastructure for these sites. They also usually grant other favourable conditions in order to attract corporations, such as exemptions from various laws, the control of unions, low rents and power charges, and exemption from most taxes, sometimes for ten or fifteen years.

The effectiveness of the Free Trade Zones is debatable.[78] They are a source of wage income, but only for a relatively few privileged workers. Some studies conclude that they are of negligible benefit to the local countries in view of the cost of the infrastructures that have to be provided, and the fact that the manufacturing corporations often import most of their inputs and do not generate much economic activity locally. Some studies even conclude that host states sometimes pay out more than they receive from the corporations. For example, according to one estimate the Bataan zone in the Philippines earned $82 million between 1973 and 1982, but cost the government $192 million.[79] As one report concludes, 'export-led development has left the poor poorer.'[80]

Tariffs

The rich countries impose import tariffs on commodities from the Third World according to the degree to which they have been processed. They might allow raw cotton to be imported without tariff, but on cotton that has been made into cloth in the Third World tariff will have to be paid, and on cotton made into clothes in the Third World a tariff which adds 20–40% to the price might be imposed. This ensures that the developed countries can carry out much of the processing, which adds most to the final or retail price. Third World suppliers of commodities receive on average only about 15% of the eventual retail prices which those commodities realise.[81] Late in the 1970s the potential earnings lost to the Third World through tariffs were estimated to total $30–33 billion p.a.[82]

In the absence of tariffs, Third World countries could easily win back much of this business from the developed countries because their labour costs are far lower. This means that through their use of tariffs and other trade barriers such as import quotas, the developed countries are directly blocking much potential Third World development. This is understandable insofar as rich countries fear that business and jobs would be lost if they lowered their tariffs, but it shows how unprepared the rich countries are to inconvenience themselves in order to enable the Third World to prosper.

Critics of conventional development point out that even if the rich countries were to remove tariffs and permit the Third World to produce all the goods it can do so more cheaply, this would be unlikely to make much difference to the welfare of most people, because it would merely enrich the few already rich people who own the exporting factories, which are often transnational corporations from the rich countries anyway. They would go on paying the lowest possible wages. There might be some small benefit arising from the new jobs created for poor people, and the increased taxes paid.

Rich world agricultural subsidies

One of the clearest grounds for Third World complaint against the rich countries centres on the very substantial subsidies the governments of the rich countries pay to their farmers, amounting to approximately $45 billion p.a. in the mid-1980s. These sums result in vast overproduction in the rich countries. They also enable the rich countries to sell large quantities of commodities which the Third World countries could otherwise supply.

Removing or at least reducing these subsidies has been a major goal of many conferences and campaigns, notably those organised by the United Nations Commission on Trade and Development. This goal is often spoken of in terms of the need to make world trade more rational and efficient. For instance, it is argued that consumers in the rich countries could have much cheaper agricultural products if the subsidies were removed and the poor countries were allowed to compete.

Yet the situation is not so simple. Those subsidies enable large numbers of people in rich countries to remain on their farms, and without them many more country towns would fade. Most developed countries already have a serious rural crisis, with many farmers going bankrupt every year. That $45 billion can be seen as relatively cheap welfare expenditure, because if the farm subsidies ceased there would be a massive flood of farm closures, and the dole queues would swell. The rural crisis in the rich countries is best seen as one consequence of an overall crisis in the world capitalist economic system. The huge subsidies to the farm sector are not irrational oversights, or mistakes that could easily be remedied.

Terms of trade

Third World countries often complain that there has been a steady decline in the amount of goods they can afford to import with their earnings from a given amount of exports. There are on record a number of periods when poor countries have suffered a significant long term decline in their terms of trade. This has been especially characteristic of the period since the early 1970s.

There have also, however, been periods in which the terms of trade have gone against the rich countries, and in the long term there does not seem to have been any significant overall trend against the Third World.[83]

Some early critical theorists, notably Prebish, Singer and Emmanuel,[84] saw falling terms of trade or 'unequal exchange' in trade as the main factors explaining the Third World's underdevelopment. Poor countries were claimed to have lost a significant proportion of their surplus wealth through these mechanisms. Although critical discussion of development often vaguely assumes that unequal exchange is the basic problem, few are now willing to attempt a defence of this position, and it is not generally accepted. Bornschier and Chase-Dunn, for instance, refer to studies finding no clear relation between trade variables and rate of development,[85] and they reject trade as the essential cause of underdevelopment. Apart from the difficulty in explaining precisely how exchange is unequal, these accounts identify stagnation due to the loss of surplus capital as the core problem. The argument in Chapter 4 and in Chapter 8 is that these are not the key concepts for understanding underdevelopment; stagnation is not occurring, despite undeniable losses of capital a lot of development is taking place, and there is quite sufficient capital for appropriate development.

No doubt there is a place for some amount of trading within a satisfactory framework of development. However, Third World countries easily find themselves drawn into far too much trade and other economic interactions with the developed countries and their corporations. It is very much in the interests of the transnational corporations and banks of the rich countries that there should be more rather than less trade. The more international business that takes place the better it is for them, and it is not surprising that conventional development theory encourages as much increase in world trade as is possible. Advocates of appropriate development strongly suggest keeping imports as low as possible, especially avoiding importing luxuries or goods that can be reasonably produced at home. Minimising imports means minimising the effort that has to go into exporting in order to pay for those imports.

Trade: Who Benefits?

'. . . we can state almost without reservation that the principal benefits of world trade have accrued disproportionate to rich nations and within poor nations disproportionately to both foreign residents and wealthy nationals'. Todaro goes on to state that trade has been harmful to many poor countries.

M. P. Todaro, *Economic Development in the Third World*, New York, Longmans, 1985, p. 393.

A glaring example of the trade trap comes from the Solomon islands.[86] At one time the islanders were highly self-sufficient, able to derive most of their food and materials from their rich forests. But then transnational corporations persuaded the government to open the islands for logging. Many islands have had their forests completely destroyed and can no longer provide for themselves, so they have to search for some other export item that might enable them to pay for imports which have become essential – and which the logging company ships bring into the company stores when they return to load up with logs! Meanwhile exposure to Western affluent life-styles has seduced the islanders into believing that they must have luxuries like TV sets, meaning that they must earn export income to pay for their increased ·import demands. They will therefore have to start competing to sell something that the rich countries want. The item they will most likely end up selling is some form of cheap labour.

Obviously it is not in our interests nor those of the corporations for those islanders to remain economically self-sufficient. We start to gain only if they can be drawn into selling us things we want, and buying things from us. A small amount of trade might have a place in appropriate development for the Solomon islanders. If one begins, as one always should, with the question 'What sort of development would be appropriate here?' the answer would focus on the maintenance of the rich forests. Any appropriate solution would minimise reliance on Western consumer goods, and would certainly keep to an absolute minimum economic entanglement with rich countries and their corporations. Yet conventional development theory contradicts these principles: it can only conceive of development in terms of becoming more affluent, industrialised, urban, 'modern', and more integrated into the global economy. Conventional development theory delivers them to us.

Finally, note again how the indiscriminate character of conventional development theory also ensures that it fails to focus on the right questions in the area of trade. It would have us believe that all is well so long as a nation is exporting at least as much as it is importing, and thus not running up a balance of trade deficit. But look what things are typically being exported and imported: luxury foods grown on the best lands are exported, and most of the resulting income goes to the rich few who own the plantations. They spend it on importing TV sets and Volvos, and some of the taxes they pay to the government are used to import relatively low protein food for those who could have been producing their own food from the land which is under export crops. These activities are highly inappropriate, yet conventional sheer growth development theory applauds them all on the grounds that any increase in business turnover, especially in trade, is a good thing.

AID

Some forms of aid are indisputably worthwhile, most obviously disaster relief and the establishment of systems and skills that will increase the capacity of poor people to provide for themselves. However, there are a number of reasons why the overall aid picture is not very inspiring.

Firstly, how much aid do we give? For every dollar the rich countries spend on themselves, they give about 3 or 4 cents in aid to the Third World, and the proportion has slowly been falling.

Most aid, moreover, is not a gift. Much of it comes in the form of a low interest loan, so it has to be repaid and therefore adds to the Third World's debt problem. This also means that the aid is not likely to go towards the most urgent or appropriate projects, because improving a village water supply for instance is not likely to produce the cash return with which the loan can be repaid. Hence the tendency will be to stimulate commercial activities, yielding only minute trickle down benefits for those in most need.

Much aid is 'tied', given on condition that it will be spent within the country granting the aid. This usually means that the recipient will derive less benefit per dollar of aid than if the dollar could have been spent purchasing the same sorts of goods from the cheapest supplier. Tied aid is therefore a means whereby a rich country's government generates more business for firms within its own borders.

Tied Aid

93% of U.S. aid is spent in the U.S. In 1980 4,000 firms in the U.S. received $1.3 billion from this source.
    M. P. Todaro, *The Economic Development of the Third World*, New York, Longmans, 1981, p. 416.

'Canada requires that at least 80% of aid be spent on Canadian goods and services.'
    L. Timberlake, *Africa in Crisis*, Earthscan, 1985, p. 37.

'Britain is one of the most expert "tyers" and even boasts that two-thirds of her aid money never actually leaves Britain.'
    New Internationalist, Oct., 1978, p. 22.

There is also a strong tendency for aid-donor countries to use their aid to secure advantages and concessions, such as trade agreements, revision of economic or political positions within the recipient countries, and military bases. A great deal of aid is military aid, much of it given to governments with repressive records. Chomsky and Herman[87] report evidence that the more repressive governments are given more aid than non-repressive governments – the logic of this is made clearer in Chapter 7.

Why is Aid Given?

'. . . the major motives of aid donors are not to increase efficiency and growth. Bilateral donors have made it clear that a primary motive is to promote the political, diplomatic, industrial and commercial interests of the country offering foreign assistance.

'For example, the Economic Support Fund of the U.S. Agency for International Development is explicitly intended to provide support to countries on the basis of U.S. political and security interests and about 40% of all U.S. bilateral aid comes from this Fund.' (p. 43)

'In practice foreign aid is doing little to promote growth in the Third World and less to alleviate poverty. In the end it appears to be doing little more than sustaining corrupt and often vicious regimes in power. . . .'

> K. Griffin, 'Doubts about aid', *IDS Bulletin*, 17, 7 April, 1986, pp. 36–45.

In giving aid the primary purpose of most capitalist governments '. . . is to preserve and defend their own economic and political interests in the recipient countries.'

> C. Payer, 'Is there a better way?', *Monthly Review*, Sept., 1982, p. 14.

'Donor countries give aid primarily because it is in their political, strategic and/or economic self-interest to do so.' p. 446

'It remains widely agreed that donor countries have utilized foreign aid largely as a political lever to prop up or underpin "friendly" political regimes in the Third World countries . . .' p. 413

> M. P. Todaro, *Economic Development in the Third World*, New York, Longmans, 1981.

'At a generous estimate only half of U.S. food aid has gone to nations hard-hit by hunger.'

> *New Internationalist*, Sept., 1979.

The American food aid programme (PL 480) was designed mainly to develop future commercial markets and to get rid of the surplus production. More than three-quarters of the aid has gone in the form of low interest credits; i.e., food sold to governments which they can then *resell*. This means the poor do not get this food. More than 90% of American food aid to Bangladesh since 1974 has been in this form; 90% of this food goes to the urban middle classes. This aid is therefore aid to client governments; a means of raising revenue and of rewarding particular groups. In many cases the money saved finances arms purchases; 85% of Korean food aid credits were used in this way in the 1960's.

'In many cases PL480 credits are not given unless the recipient government agrees to expand commercial imports from the U.S.'

Derived from R. Burbach and P. Flynn, *Agribusiness in the Americas*, 1980, p. 65.

'The great bulk of loans to the Third World nations has gone to approximately a dozen countries whose dictatorships have provided optimum conditions for foreign capital at the expense of their people.'

G. McCormack, 'The South Korean Phenomenon', *Australian Outlook*, 32,3, Dec., 1978, p. 279.

After we have separated out all the cynical and manipulative uses of aid, we find the core problem: most of the remainder is intended to stimulate conventional development. Hence large sums go into big infrastructure projects such as dams and power grids, and into promoting normal commercial ventures, such as export crops. These uses of aid would make sense if significant trickle down could be expected from the development they facilitate. In general, however, these projects have mostly benefited the richer few, especially people who live in the cities. They are usually the only people able to afford the electricity the dams produce.

Does Most Aid Go to the Poorest?

Is aid given mostly to the poorest? In 1980 OECD aid to the 31 LDCs averaged $4.75 per capita, while aid from this group to the richest Third World countries averaged $5.78 per capita.

> J. Loup, *Can the Third World Survive?* 1980, p. 38.

'In 1981 Israel's GNP per head was nearly 37 times larger than Ethiopia's, yet Israel received 90 times more foreign capital per head than Ethiopia.'

> K. Griffin, 'Doubts about aid', *IDS Bulletin*, 17,7, April, 1986, p. 39.

The 'brain drain': reverse aid?

Many professional people migrate from poor to rich countries. In 1972, 44,843 entered the USA, Canada and Britain to live permanently.[88] If the cost of educating these people is taken into account it can be seen as aid worth several billion dollars p.a. flowing from poor to rich countries.

Can aid solve the problems?

Many existing forms of aid are undoubtedly desirable, and in a humane world rich countries could be of immense assistance to the Third World, but the main conclusion the foregoing discussion comes to is that *aid is not very important as a solution to the Third World's problems.* These problems are mainly due to the unjust way in which the global economy works. No significant progress can be made until the rich countries come to accept a drastic redistribution of wealth and power, and cease gearing so much of the Third World's productive capacity to the rich world interests. *It is not that the rich world should give more, but that they should take less.*

LOANS

In the 1970s rich world banks loaned a great deal of money to Third World countries, mainly because they had accumulated large sums from the oil-rich countries following the price rises of the early 1970s. This eagerness to lend, coupled with the recession that commenced in the 1970s, has been a major factor leading to the serious Third World debt problem. Loans have to be repaid, plus interest. Because the level of debt has risen so high, and because interest rates have also been high, in the early 1980s the amount of money that Third World countries have had to repay to the rich countries each year has actually been far greater than the amount of money being lent to them each year. In 1985 the Third World's repayments of loans and interest amounted to $30 billion more than the loans it received in that year. In 1986 it received $14 billion in aid, but it paid out $54 billion in loan repayments plus interest.[89] Over the period 1982–1985 it paid back $106 billion more than it received.

As with trade and foreign investment, loans in themselves are not necessarily undesirable. The problem is that in a global economy where the emphasis is on maximising the return on investment, there is a strong tendency for loans to go into ventures most unlikely to meet basic needs.

Loans for what?

'. . . the people who lend the money need to be paid commercial rates. So World Bank projects tend to be those that will quickly generate the necessary foreign exchange. There is, therefore, a heavy emphasis on export industries – even if this means, for example, sweeping local Indian tribes aside in order to export the timber from their forests.'

New Internationalist, Feb., 1987, p. 11.

IMF 'RESTRUCTURING'

When Third World countries get into serious financial difficulties, as many do, the International Monetary Fund 'rescues' them. It assists in rescheduling debt payments and organising new loans to get a country over a crisis period, but in the process it insists on changes in economic policies. This restructuring or stabilisation is designed 'to get the economy going again' in conventional terms, which mainly means cutting spending and increasing export earnings in order to start paying off the debt.

The standard IMF rescue package includes reducing government spending on welfare and subsidies on food and housing, holding down or cutting wages, giving the green light to free enterprise, encouraging foreign investment, deflating and restricting credit, and devaluing the currency, thus making exports more competitive. All these measures impose increased hardships on the poor. They redistribute wealth and opportunities to the rich who have capital to invest, because the point of the exercise is to encourage them to generate more economic activity, especially exports. As Murdoch says, '. . . it is an explicit and basic aim of IMF programs to discourage local consumption in order to free resources for exports.'[90] Hence 'getting the economy going again' involves devoting more resources to producing for export to the rich world and charging less for these items (because of devaluation), again redistributing productive capacity to the benefit of the rich. Similarly, the recent move to 'debt for equity' swaps and the IMF's pressure for privatisation both help to transfer the ownership of more productive capacity to foreign banks and corporations.[91]

Local firms also suffer because measures such as restricting credit can devastate small businesses. Transnational corporations are then in a good position to move in and take over these business opportunities. Measures such as these may succeed in 'getting the economy going' (though there is debate about their effectiveness even in these narrow terms), but the cost is borne by those least able to afford it. As Payer says, 'The costs in human terms of these stabilisation programs are enormous.[92] In fact the protests which these policies have evoked from poor people who have seen food prices rise and their welfare and subsidies cut had led to the term 'IMF riots'.

The resulting stimulus to the economy is mainly effective in increasing exports and making foreign investment more attractive. The package is therefore a delight to transnational corporations and consumers in rich countries, but it produces anything but development in the interests of Third World people.

Much critical comment has been directed at these IMF stabilisation strategies. Michael Manley, Prime Minister of Jamaica, said 'IMF prescriptions are designed by and for the developed capitalist countries and are inappropriate for developing countries of any kind.'[93] The IMF, not surprisingly, is controlled by the rich countries, especially by the USA.

Why do poor countries put up with such treatment? Because the IMF determines their credit ratings. If the IMF says that you are not a sound customer, you will not be able to borrow from anyone.

Again it is important to understand that what is going on here is not necessarily a deliberate restructuring intended to advantage the corporations and the rich countries at the expense of the poor. These actions mainly derive from conventional economic theory which points to them as the way 'go get the economy going', and which holds as supremely important the ability to earn lots of export income and thus raise the GNP. The very same theory leads to the same policies even in the richest countries, where the poor are obliged to restrain wage demands and pull in their belts in order to make investment more profitable, so that those with capital might be tempted to invest it and generate more economic turnover. In our economic system, capitalists always come first in the queue; if it does not suit them to invest, they leave their money in the bank (earning interest), productive capacity sits idle, and the rest of us have to get by with insufficient goods and jobs.

FOOD AND AGRICULTURE

Now let us look at what happens in relation to food and agriculture when market forces are allowed to become major determinants of development.

In the 1960s and 1970s the Green Revolution came to Third World agriculture. New varieties of grains were developed and new techniques were introduced, resulting in considerable increases in yields. These developments were associated with the 'modernisation of agriculture', the movement from traditional peasant methods of production to those used on large Western farms. Modern agriculture involves heavy use of fertilizers, pesticides, irrigation, technical advice and transport, all of which are intensive energy users. It is therefore not surprising that oil corporations are central among the big agribusiness corporations that now dominate the field.

The modernisation of Third World agriculture also means the increasing commercialisation of food production. Whereas much food used to be produced on small plots, not for sale but for immediate local consumption, there has recently been an acceleration in areas planted by agribusiness transnational corporations, producing food for cash sale in a market, frequently an export market. These developments represent a rapid shift towards food production and supply systems governed by market forces.

There is no doubt that overall output in many regions has been considerably increased by Green Revolution technology. Rice yields may have risen 25% and wheat yields by up to 70%.[94] In the 1980s India was able to boast that it had become a grain exporter. But there are heated debates about the net effects of the modernisation of agriculture and the Green Revolution.

First, the modernisation of Third World agriculture has brought increased dependence on imported energy, especially as agriculture mostly requires the scarcest form of energy, liquid fuel. It has also increased dependence on imported technology, inputs and capital, and on foreign markets and economic conditions. In other words, the modernisation of agriculture represents a significant jump in the opposite direction to that being argued for by appropriate development theorists, who advocate independence and regional self-sufficiency regarding inputs and marketing, reliance on local inputs, and avoidance of chemical fertilizers and non-renewable forms of energy.

The modernisation of agriculture has a strong tendency to enrich the few richer landowners, because they are the ones who can afford to risk trying the new seeds, and who can afford the costly inputs that the seeds must have if they are to do well. These farmers often prosper and buy out poorer farmers or terminate peasant leases in order to expand their cropped areas. Hence the modernisation of agriculture has been a major factor contributing to the growing numbers of landless peasants and the drift to urban slums.

In addition, the produce from modern farming is inevitably more expensive than that from traditional methods of farming because the cost of the expensive inputs has to be covered. Consequently the majority of poor people are often unable to afford to buy the food produced, and it tends to be sent to the cities or overseas where buyers are more affluent. Hence modernising agriculture can mean little more than converting land from production by the poor for use by the poor, to production by rich farmers for use by the rich in the Third World and by consumers in the rich world.

There is therefore a clash between the interests of poor farmers and their communities on the one hand, and on the other the interests of the rich, the transnational corporations and the consumers in rich countries. Agribusiness corporations want to sell tractors, pesticides, fertilizers and irrigation equipment, and to sell high-priced produce in the most affluent markets where the most profit can be made. The poor majority, however, would be much better served by agricultural development which required few imported inputs and was not geared to distant markets. Several people have argued that for these reasons the modernisation of agriculture may have actually increased the amount of hunger in many parts of the Third World. There is certainly extensive evidence on the way it has reduced the welfare of large numbers of people, by making them landless, by raising prices, or by diverting food that was available locally to distant markets.

Green Revolution: More Food or More Hunger?

Recent green revolution increases in food production in the poor countries have actually resulted in an increase in hunger, because the new technology has been brought into iniquitous social structures which have enabled the rich to become much richer and to dispossess the poor.

'The lure of greater profits tempts large landlords to take back land they formerly rented out. Many use their now higher profits to buy out small neighbouring famers.' 30 to 60% of rural people are now landless.

'We are thus witnessing the radical transformation of the control of food resources . . . Agriculture, once the livelihood for millions of self-provisioning farmers in the Third World, is being turned into a profit base for a new class of "farmers". In the course of this transformation the hungry are being severed from the production process. At best they become insecure wage labourers with seasonal jobs. To be cut out of the production process is to be cut out of consumption.

'There is more food, but people are still hungry – in fact, more hungry. The process of creating more food has actually reduced people's ability to grow or to buy food.'

F. M. Lappe and J. Collins, 'More food means more hunger', *Futurist*, xi,2, April, 1977, 90–93.

'. . . the experience of the "green revolution" suggests that this strategy has actually worked against the rural poor. It has led to a reduction in tenancy and a swelling of the ranks of landless wage-labourers.'

K. Ajit and K. Griffin, 'Rural poverty and development alternatives . . .', IFDA *Dossier* 9, July, 1979, p. 6.

'I think it is safe to conclude that . . . in important respects [the green revolution] has intensified rather than helped alleviate the problems associated with feeding the world's rising numbers.'

M. Caldwell, *The Wealth of Some Nations*, 1977, p. 41.

'The Green Revolution bolstered inequalities, and numerous studies established that increased food production often exacerbated hunger.'

Far Eastern Economic Review, 13th July, 1979, p. 39.

'. . . more food is being produced, yet more people are hungry. International Labor Organisation studies document that in the very Asian countries – Pakistan, India, Bangladesh, Sri Lanka, Malaysia, the Philippines and Indonesia – where the Green Revolution has been pushed, and where, indeed, food production per person has risen, the rural poor are worse off than before.'

'Other studies by the United Nations Research Institute for Social Development confirm the pattern; in the Third World, on the whole, there is more food and less to eat.'

Collins, J., and F. M. Lappe, 'Still hungry after all these years', *Mother Jones*, Aug., 1977.

This issue also adds to the argument that the main need is not for technical solutions which will permit greater production. The food and hunger problem is basically due not to any shortage of food, but to the unsatisfactory distribution of food and food producing resources which result when market forces are allowed to determine agricultural development. The need is for better social and economic arrangements so that the available food-producing capacity can be geared to the needs of the majority of people.

The growth of export cropping

Closely related to the modernisation of Third World agriculture has been the rapid increase in the areas producing crops for sale in the cities or for export to rich countries. The Third World exports more food to the rich countries (20.2% of world food traded in 1976) than it imports from them (12% of world food traded in 1976).[95] In addition the food exported to the rich countries is generally of higher quality. Their imports are mostly of grain, but their exports include peanuts, vegetables, fruit and meat, and many luxuries like coffee, strawberries and flowers.

Areas planted for cash or export crops have been increasing much faster than those planted for local consumption; perhaps twice as fast. In many poor countries more than half of the best land now produces export crops.[96]

The Increase in Export Crops

Dammann estimates that 110 million acres of Third World land grow crops for export to rich countries. 'For the cultivation of coffee, tea and cocoa alone, the rich countries use about 40 million acres in the Third World.'

E. Dammann, *Future in Our Hands*, 1979, p. 95.

In Central America, where half the children are maln-

---

ourished, 50% of the land is used to produce crops
for export. Mexican land can yield 12 times the profit
resulting from producing food for local consumption
if it is put into production of tomatoes for export to
the U.S.

In Central America 80 times as much is made on
export of carnations as would be made if the land was
put into food production.

> P. Adamson, Editor of *The New Internationalist*,
> speaking on ABC Guest of Honour programme,
> 4th June, 1977.

'In Haiti, one of the poorest countries in the world,
the mountain slopes are ravaged by hungry peasants,
while the rich valleys are devoted to low-nutrition and
feed crops – sugar, coffee, cocoa, alfalfa for cattle
– for export. Recently, the Institute for Food and
Development Policy reports, United States firms have
been flying Texas cattle into the island, fattening them
up there, and then re-exporting them to American-
franchised hamburger restaurants.

So the poor countries make a major contribution to
the diet of the rich. And the rich want to keep it that
way.' '. . . the logic of the world market makes it
"sensible" for a country to let its people hunger while
it fattens up foreigners.'

> M. Harrington, *The Vast Majority*, 1977, p. 157.

In Senegal a subsidiary of the giant American transnational Bud Antle '. . . has established huge irrigated
"garden plantations" on land from which peasants
have been removed. These plantations produce
vegetables in the winter and feed for livestock (for
export) in the summer. *None of this produce is eaten in
Senegal*. . . .

'This process is occurring across all of North Africa.
In Ethiopia in an area where thousands of people

were evicted to make way for agribusiness and then starved to death, international firms are producing alfalfa to feed livestock in Japan. . . . during the Sahelian famine the acreage planted to groundnuts in Senegal was increasing, while that planted to sorghum and millet for local consumption was actually decreasing.[97]

W. Murdoch, *The Poverty of Nations*, Baltimore, Johns Hopkins University Press, 1980, pp. 297–298.

'Conditions in the countryside lie at the heart of the intensifying class conflict in El Salvador. The capitalist transformation of agriculture has led to a situation of crisis proportions for the 60% of Salvadoreans who live in rural areas. With the spread of export crop production in the post-war period, tens of thousands of peasants were displaced from their lands. Today, three major export crops – coffee, cotton, and sugar – dominate the lands formerly tilled by subsistence farmers, and 60% of the land owned by only 2% of the population.

'. . . hunger on a mass scale is a direct result of the production of agricultural goods for profit rather than for human need.

'Where the majority of people are too poor to make their basic needs felt in the marketplace, the food-producing resources serve those who can pay – the privileged elite within the country and higher paying foreign markets. Thus food-producing resources that could be feeding hungry people are misused for the already adequately fed.

'In the Caribbean where as many as 80 percent of the children are undernourished, about 44 percent of the land, invariably the best land, is used to grow just four export crops: coffee, bananas, cocoa, and sugar cane, which serve to enrich a small domestic elite.'

Food First Resource Guide, IFDP, 1979, p. 9.

'For as far as the eye can see the rolling fields of
southern Mindanao are blanketed with banana trees.
No Filipino will ever eat them, only Japan's
consumers and Angus cattle.'
Far Eastern Economic Review, July 13, 1979, p. 51.

During the early 1970's Sahelian drought enough
grain was being produced to feed everyone, but '. . .
even during the worst drought years there was an
increase in agricultural exports from the Sahel –
cotton and peanuts in particular.'
Self Reliance for a Small Planet, IDFP Pamphlet,
1980, p. 4.

Export cropping can be seen as one of the most
disturbing outcomes of the conventional approach to development. This approach encourages poor countries to
devote much of their land to those export crops giving
them a 'comparative advantage' in order to earn income
to be spent on imports. But this means that huge areas of
Third World land end up growing luxury crops for overfed
people in the rich countries, while the people who work in
the plantations go hungry. That land should be planted by
local malnourished people in order to feed themselves.
Little of the money earned by exporting food ends up
benefiting poor people. Much of it is spent by rich plantation owners to purchase luxuries, and the proportion
going to the government in taxes (which is often negligible)
is spent mostly on development which is of little benefit to
the majority of people.

Export cropping represents perhaps the most important
form of wealth transfer from the poor to the rich. Most of
the wealth created by labour in the plantations goes to
enrich corporations and consumers in rich countries. We
would pay much more for our coffee and tea if the people
who produced these and other commodities in the Third
World received adequate wages, or if most of that land was

growing basic food for them. Often they receive something like 2% of the retail value of the commodities they produce, and their wages might be one-twentieth of ours in real terms. They work hard to produce wealth but they end up with a minute fraction of it, and this constitutes a vast transfer of wealth from them to us.

The export cropping phenomenon is probably the most glaringly repugnant consequence of the conventional approach to development. There can be a place for export crops in appropriate development strategies, especially where smallholders can earn a surplus to augment living standards based mainly on household or village self-sufficiency. But at present most export cropping means that tens of millions of the best Third World hectares have been stolen. They should be producing to feed the hungry people who live nearby or who actually work on them, but they have been taken over for the production of food for people who are already well fed, and for the enrichment of a very few already rich landowners and corporations.

An easily overlooked item in the global food account, similar to export cropping, is the food that rich countries secure by means of their fishing fleets. Rich countries have fishing boats taking most of the fish from the coasts of very poor and hungry countries. Borgstrom[98] has calculated that the food value of the fish consumed in Holland in the early 1960s was equal to that produced by 13 million acres of land. Holland's own farmland totalled only 7.9 million acres. Borgstrom refers to this vast 'ghost acreage' which the rich countries have at their command. In addition, the area of land which was producing food imported into Holland at that time was 12 million acres.

The Economics of Hunger

'Another result of marketing food on the basis of profitability is to divert food products from the country where they are grown and needed to those

which can offer higher prices . . . For example, the fish
meal industry of Chile and Peru is owned primarily by
American and Western European interests. Nearly
half the protein taken from the Pacific comes from the
fisheries off the coasts of Chile and Peru. Almost all
the fish taken are converted into animal feed in the
fish meal factories in these countries. Nearly the entire
output of fish meal is exported to Western Europe,
the United States and Japan. Yet the rate of malnutrition in Peru is one of the worst in Latin America.
It is preposterous that the two most protein-needy
continents, Africa and South America, are the
suppliers of the largest quantity of animal protein feed
in world trade.'

R. Dennis and R. Landsness, *The Economics of
Hunger*, (1978)

Why is there a food and hunger problem?

Third World governments have tended to neglect agriculture and rural regions. Most attention has been given to
industrial development, and the rural sector has often been
squeezed economically to accumulate capital for the industrial sector. This is understandable given that industrialisation has been seen as the key to rapid economic growth.
In addition governments are under much more political
pressure to deliver benefits to their more organised and
articulate urban sectors. But these are not the most
important reasons for the problem.

We have seen that hunger and malnutrition are not due
to insufficient food production or insufficient arable land.
The problem is that large numbers of people are unable to
buy available food or do not have access to the land which
would enable them to produce the food they need. The
main causes of hunger are poverty and social injustice.

Deliberately Unused Land

The giant U.S. corporation Del Monte owns 57,000 acres of Guatemala but plants only 9,000 acres. This prevents the peasants from using the land to grow food.

F. M. Lappe and J. Collins, *Food First*, 1977, c. 104.

'Deliberate underutilisation of land is a phenomenon of the capitalist system. Plantation owners have a vested interest in securing as much available land as possible, not so much to use it, as neo-classical economics suggests, but rather to withhold it from use, thereby ensuring their perpetuation as a class and the plantation system as a whole. The association between under utilisation of land and labour is evident everywhere in the plantation world. . . .'

L. Bondestam, 'The politics of food on the periphery', in V. Harle, *The Political Economy of Food*, 1978, p. 241.

The argument in the preceding sections has been that the main factor explaining the serious Third World food and hunger problem is the market system. Richer people can and do easily outbid poor people for food and food producing resources. Huge numbers are hungry simply because it is more profitable for the available food to be sold to richer people, who want and can afford luxuries like coffee and flowers. The market pays no attention to need. The hunger of four hundred million, or is it fourteen hundred million, is totally irrelevant. If most money can be made producing carnations to airfreight to European supermarkets, or fattening cattle to airfreight to US hamburger chains, then in a market system that is what will be done. The conclusion we come to again and again is that there is no possibility of solving basic problems like hunger until we move away from an economic system which operates on these principles.

CHAPTER 6

The Limits to Growth Perspective: Neglected Implications for Development

The argument so far has been that satisfactory development is not taking place. We come now to the argument that even if it were, change to a fundamentally different conception of development is demanded by the limits to growth predicament we now find ourselves in.[99] A vast literature on this theme has accumulated since the 1960s, but it is remarkable that development theorists have paid very little attention to it. *If the limits to growth argument is valid it totally destroys conventional assumptions about the goals of development.*

It has consistently been assumed that development is about moving to the levels of industrialisation, economic activity, resource use and especially to the affluent living standards of the 'developed' countries. The limits to growth argument emphatically conclude that there is no chance of all people achieving such goals, and that unless rich as well as poor countries abandon them in the near future a variety of global catastrophies is likely to occur.

The core of the argument is that the pursuit of affluent living standards and economic growth has led to *over-development* in the few richest countries, and that continued pursuit of these goals will produce accelerating problems of resource and energy scarcity, environmental destruction, conflict and social breakdown. The rich countries have an unsustainable way of life. They must in time make a transition to a much less affluent and more self-sufficient 'conserver' way of life, in a zero growth economy with an average per capita resource use and GNP much lower than they have at present.

THE AFFLUENT LIFESTYLES OF THE RICH COUNTRIES

Remember, only one-fifth of the world's people live in the rich countries but we are using up about four-fifths of the world's annual resource output, at a per capita rate seventeen times that enjoyed by half the world's people. These rates are partly due to high levels of unnecessary, luxurious and wasteful personal consumption. Over twenty tonnes of new materials are produced for each US citizen every year. The energy needed to produce the cans and bottles for the hundred million Cokes drunk each day throughout the world is equal to about 22,000 tonnes of coal, more than the entire country of Malawi uses for all purposes.[100]

Even more important than the volume of our unnecessary personal consumption is the fact that we have many unnecessarily expensive systems – for example to supply food. Our agriculture is one of the most clearly unsustainable characteristics of our way of life, firstly because it mines and destroys the soil, especially through erosion and non-return of nutrients, and secondly because it is so heavily dependent on non-renewable energy. A lot of energy is used on the farm, but seven times as much may be used between the farm gate and your table, mostly in transport. Where did your breakfast come from? The average US food item has been estimated to have travelled 1,300 km![101]

Then there is all the energy that goes into freezing, preserving, packaging, and lighting the supermarket. If we simply re-zoned urban wasteland for market gardens and planted our parks with 'edible landscapes' (see Chapter 9) we could probably cut the cost of food by over 70%.[102]

This figure indicates the general scale of the monetary and resource costs that could be saved if we changed to more sensible systems.

Similar arguments apply to housing, water supply, sewage systems and decentralisation. We have incredibly expensive sewerage systems for taking household wastes and throwing them away, requiring scarce energy for pumping, when all those nutrients should be returned to the soil. Our agriculture is in effect 'soil mining', the nutrients in each crop being taken from the soil and thrown away after one use. You cannot go on doing that for very long, yet it would not be difficult to change to systems

whereby all those nutrients could be recycled to domestic gardens and local market gardens (see Chapter 9).

If our workplaces were decentralised, fewer cars would be needed because many of us could then get to work by bicycle or on foot. The vast expense of dams, mains and pumping for our domestic water supply could be greatly reduced if more rainwater was collected from house roofs.

RESOURCE IMPLICATIONS

Unless existing estimates of all potentially recoverable mineral and energy resources (including all the deposits we are ever likely to find) are gross underestimates, there is no chance that everybody in the world can rise to anywhere near the per capita use rates that the few in rich countries enjoy now.'[103]

World population is likely to rise to perhaps eleven billion late next century. If all of those people were each to consume as much energy as people in rich countries do now, world annual energy production would have to be ten times as great as it is at present. Figure 7 shows that present estimates of potentially recoverable conventional fuels could never bring us to that level, let alone maintain it for any length of time. Those who suggest that this might be achieved using nuclear energy should be aware that it would require the building of 200,000 giant reactors, one thousand times the world's present nuclear capacity. It would also require ways of running everything by electricity, which constitutes only about 12% of US end-use energy at present.

Nor is there any foreseeable way of deriving such enormous quantities of energy from alternative sources such as the sun, wind or tides.[104] A sustainable alternative society will be based on these alternative sources, but only at per capita use rates which are a small fraction of present average energy use rates in the rich countries.

Figure 8 sets out the scale of the problem, assuming that the Third World rises to present American per capita

Figure 7: If All Have Our Energy Use?

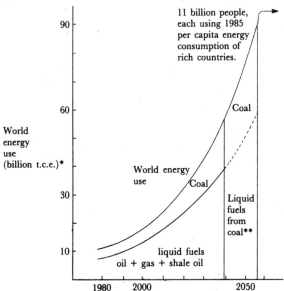

* t.c.e. = tonne of coal equivalent in energy
** Assuming 65% energy efficiency of conversation process

Conclusion: All probably recoverable resources of conventional fuels (excluding alternatives, breeders and fusion) will be *totally exhaused by 2057*.
(Assumed quantities, in t.c.e.: oil 314b, gas 390b, shale oil 1416b, coal 2000b, uranium 157b; total 4277b; see Trainer, 1985, Chapter 4)

energy use and that world population grows to eleven billion. This would mean that total energy use late next century would have to be *fourteen times* what it is now. (These exercises ignore possible increases in per capita energy use in rich countries: a 1% p.a. increase would mean twice as much consumed by each individual in 2050 as in 1980, a 2% p.a. increase would mean four times as much.)

Unless you are prepared to make wild assumptions about resources and technology, the inescapable conclusion is that *there is no chance of all people in the world living as affluently as people in the rich countries do at present*. We are the *overdeveloped* countries and the rest are the *never-to-be-developed* countries. We can only remain as affluent as we are if we go on

Figure 8: Present American per capita energy use for 11 billion people

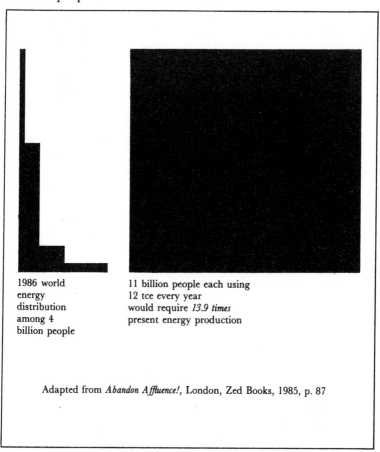

1986 world energy distribution among 4 billion people

11 billion people each using 12 tce every year would require *13.9 times* present energy production

Adapted from *Abandon Affluence!*, London, Zed Books, 1985, p. 87

taking far more than our fair share of the dwindling resources, and if the poor majority remain far below our consumption rates.

It follows that a sustainable, just and peaceful world order will be impossible to achieve unless the rich countries move to lifestyles and systems which enable them to consume far less of the world's resources. They must learn to live on something like their fair share. At first sight this conclusion might be disturbing, but it will be argued in Chapter 9 that there are alternative technologies and forms of social organisation which would enable us to live on very low levels of resource and energy consumption while actually enjoying a higher quality of life than most of us have now.

But let us for a moment imagine that it was possible to sustain fourteen times the present world energy output, and therefore to lift all people to the present living standards of the rich countries. In the mid-1970s about 10% of people in the rich countries were still living under the poverty line. This would mean that in a world of eleven billion, living as we do now, 1,100 million people would still be living in poverty! How much more growth would be needed to solve this problem? The outlook is even more nonsensical when we recognise that periods of growth often do not see welfare conditions improve. In the decade to 1985 the GNP of rich countries increased by 30%, but in general the incidence of unemployment and poverty became *greater*.

ENVIRONMENTAL IMPACT

In achieving our high levels of production and consumption we are doing enormous and increasing damage to the ecosystems of the planet. We burn five billion tonnes of fuel every year (most of it in the overdeveloped countries), releasing gases which are likely to bring about a 'greenhouse effect', a warming of the globe's atmosphere which is predicted to raise sea levels a possible 140cm by the year 2030, and to disrupt agriculture. The only way we can avoid such effects is by drastically reducing energy production and consumption.

Tropical rainforest is being destroyed at fifteen million hectares p.a., and will probably be largely non-existent by 2040.[105] This involves the destruction of habitats, and species of plants and animals are being lost at the rate of perhaps one a day at present, likely to accelerate to 150 a

'Wouldn't it be better to stop him?'

day in fifteen years' time.[106] This means that after having eliminated perhaps three hundred species in the last three centuries, human activity could eliminate *one million* in the next two decades.

The most important impetus to this destruction is the drive to increase production and consumption in the already over-producing rich countries. More than 40% of the Brazilian forest lost in recent years has been due to clearing for cattle production, mainly for export to US fast food outlets.[107]

If the economies of the rich countries grow at a mere 3% p.a. until 2050, their annual economic output will then be about *eight times* what it is now. A 5% p.a. rate of growth would mean *32 times* the present annual output by 2050. Unless totally unforeseen developments take place in impact reduction, the implications of significant economic growth for global ecosystems must be catastrophic.

Those who would seek to shrug off these arguments by assuming that technical advance will solve the problems have considerable difficulties to confront, most importantly the fact that in most of the crucial areas the technology is falling behind the mounting problems.[108] The long term production costs of minerals and energy are rising, especially the energy and capital costs of their production.[109] Major food yields, notably world grain yield and fish production, are falling despite steeply increasing inputs.[110]

THE PROBLEM OF PEACE

A global economic system delivering most wealth to the rich few, who are determined to go on endlessly becoming richer although most people in the world are deprived, while world population is set to double by 2050, when the Third World will outnumber the rich world by 6 or 8 to 1, while resources are becoming more scarce and give no possibility of all people ever rising to the present living

standards of the rich countries – can only see the emergence of more and more conflict in many forms.[111]

Conventional development strategies exacerbate the peace problem in two main ways. The first is by generating the inequality and maldistribution which produce much of the violence in the world, especially the 'structural' violence of 43,000 infant deaths wrought by deprivation every day and the class war waged by Third World elites. The second is by obliging the major beneficiaries of the system, the developed countries and their transnational corporations, to engage in the vast military preparation needed to secure the empire against dissent from within (indigenous revolution) and threat from without (subversion or attack).

The implication for those who would seek a more peaceful world is that their goal is not likely to be achieved unless and until appropriate development strategies are adopted or permitted, providing for a radical redistribution of world wealth and fundamental changes in living standards within rich countries both East and West.

OUR FALLING QUALITY OF LIFE

Even if none of the preceding resource or environment problems existed, we would still have strong reasons for abandoning the quest for endlessly rising affluence and GNP. How many people in the richest countries would claim that their average quality of life is now improving? Several indicators suggest that it is in fact falling, and that this is due to the same forces which are generating the resource, environment, Third World and other problems.

Most if not all social problems are getting worse: crime, vandalism, homelessness, alcoholism, stress diseases, depression, analgesic consumption, the hard drug problem and child abuse. Most of these phenomena reflect social breakdown and discontent with personal circumstances. Add to the list noise, traffic congestion, pollution, pace, distance to travel to work, urban blight, and poverty. According to some measures poverty rates in some rich countries, such as Australia, have doubled in the last decade.

Surveys asking people how they feel about their lives find that levels of satisfaction are either the same as they were ten or twenty years ago, or are considerably lower. Easterlin, for example, reviewed thirty studies and found no relation between contentment and change in GNP over time.[112] American quality of life response rates in 1970 were much the same as in 1940, although their real per capita incomes had doubled in that time. Americans do not enjoy life three times as much as the Irish, or ten times as much as Cubans, or 66 times as much as Burmese, as they should if the level of GNP determined one's quality of life. The percentage of Americans who say they are happy is about the same as the percentage of Cubans, and it is probably lower than the number of Burmese.[113]   Australian real income per person has approximately trebled since World War II: are Australians three times as contented now?

There are good reasons for thinking that contrary to the conventional assumption, raising the GP directly *lowers* the quality of life in the overdeveloped countries. The more we commercialise our lives the more we whittle away those non-economic social relationships which ensure a warm and supportive community spirit. Three hundred years ago the market had only a very minor place in our society. Very few things were produced for sale, and cost-benefit calculations did not determine what things were produced, or by whom, or how they changed hands. Land was not sold, and capital could not be lent for interest. There was no labour market. Decisions about who was to work for whom and at what wage were made according to social rules, not left to market forces. Tradition, religion, and morality determined social interaction, not the market.

But we now leave most things for the market to settle, and market calculations are essentially selfish rather than communal or social. People look for what will maximise their self interest rather than what is best for society, and there is no scope for a collective decision as to what is the most socially beneficial course of action. As time goes by we are allowing commerce and the market to determine even more aspects of our society. We have recently seen rapid increases in the percentage of food bought rather than prepared or grown at home; we now have laundromats and far fewer repairs are done at home than a generation ago. We buy just about everything, especially services. Communities of ordinary people tend not to get together to provide their own entertainment, education, advice, child care, care of the aged, nursing, or local government.

Various historians, notably Polanyi and Marx, have stressed this shift to market relations. Polanyi points out that no society in human history other than our own has allowed the market to become so overwhelmingly influential. All previous societies have confined the market to a very minor role. Polanyi sees this change as so significant that he entitled his book *The Great Transformation*, and he regards it as having been a dreadful mistake.[114]

The most serious consequence of allowing commerce and the market to determine so much is surely the current status of 'community'. Most people now live as rather isolated nuclear families without much access to support from extended family or local community. Many of us have almost nothing to do with our neighbours, and there are few if any activities that we become involved in within our local area. We do not have many civic responsibilities. We tend not to experience much solidarity, or feeling of identity, or commitment with respect to our local areas. Many aged, ill and handicapped people must either suffer boredom or enter a 'home'.

One way of summarising our sorry situation is to say that *we have lost our tribe*. People still living in 'primitive' hunter-gatherer societies do not have these problems. They always have familiar caring people around to talk to or to ask for help. They have a community to belong to and work for and be protected by. Many people have suggested that we in the overdeveloped countries have an urgent need to 'retribalise'.

Let us in the light of these issues now reconsider the blundering arrogance of 'modernisation' theory. It asserts that 'development' has to involve giving up tribal and village ways and satisfaction with low material living standards in order to adopt the competitive, individualistic, alienated, stress-ridden and insatiably greedy lifestyles of the overdeveloped countries.

This is certainly not to endorse all aspects of tribal or village life, but some of the most important clues for our sanity and survival are to be found within the tribe and the village. It is especially from these sources that we can relearn the right attitudes to the environment, material possessions, and community.

OUR ECONOMY: BASIC SOURCE OF THE PREDICAMENT

There is no possibility of solving 'limits to growth' problems while retaining the present economic system. This system *generates* the problems under discussion. The point is most easily driven home by a glance at the issue of waste. The over-developed countries are extraordinarily wasteful. They produce mountains of things that are totally unnecessary and they elaborate necessary items with wrappings and trimmings and built-in obsolescence. But – if we ceased producing these things in our present economy there would be chaos! Unemployment rates would jump and firms would go bankrupt if we started identifying things we don't need and ceasing to produce and consume them. If sales stagnate, let alone drop a little, there is panic, yet we are already doing far more work, producing and consuming than is necessary to maintain quite satisfactory living standards.

It is totally impossible for this economy to adjust to saner levels. It is crucial for the health of our present economy that we keep on producing all the unnecessary luxurious and wasteful things we now produce. *It is an*

Adapted from *Abandon Affluence!*, London, Zed Books, 1985, p. 239

economy which requires vast waste. If you find you can produce and sell any new product, however wasteful and unnecessary, economists and politicians will applaud because it will generate more jobs and turnover and 'help the economy recover'.

The limits to growth argument is that for reasons of sheer survival we must move to far lower levels of production, consumption and resource use, but it is clearly impossible to move in that direction with our present economic system. This economy is only healthy if the amount of producing and consuming going on constantly increases.

These contradictions exist essentially because this is a capitalist economy. People with capital want to invest it. For each dollar they invest they usually end up with $1.10 or more at the end of the year. They then want to invest all this, and they can't unless the economy expands. Last year it could accommodate a certain amount of capital investment but this year there's 10% more capital to be invested. Capitalism is about constant *accumulation.* You don't make money to spend while remaining at a stable level of operations or wealth. You strive to get richer and richer, in order to have more money to invest, to make more money, so that you can invest it to make even more money . . . If you are a manager and you refuse to do this, your shareholders will fire you.

And what shape would the world be in by 2050 given our economy's commitment to growth? Remember that a mere 3% p.a. growth rate would by then have raised output to 8 times present levels, and a 5% rate would mean 32 times as much.

Hence this economy's major and irremediable fault is its drive to overproduce and waste at an ever-increasing rate. The limits to growth argument concludes that we must work towards an economy that is not only a no-growth economy, but which operates on a far lower per capita level of production and a far lower GNP than we have now in rich countries.

A second way in which this economy generates our major

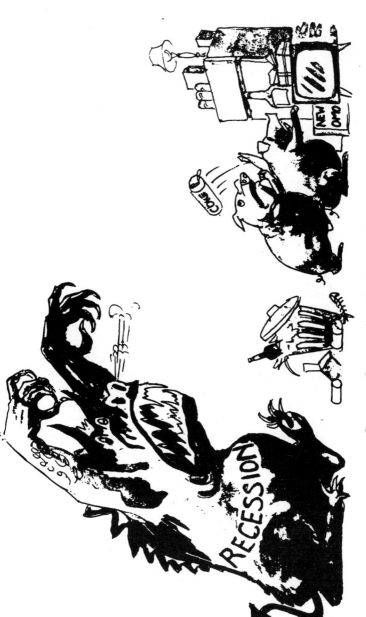

Consume faster or it will gain on us!!

problems is through *its inability to do what most needs doing*. It systematically and inevitably refuses to feed the hungry and provide for the impoverished. This economy will always attend to the rich and ignore the poor, because it is driven by profit maximisation: most profit can always be made by catering to those with more money.

Conventional wisdom claims that freedom of enterprise and the profit motive produce efficiency. They do – because conventional economic theory conveniently defines efficiency in precisely the way those with capital to invest would wish; i.e. as maximising the rate of return on invested capital. But if efficiency is defined in terms of applying existing productive capacity to meeting existing human needs, then it becomes obvious how appallingly inefficient our economic system is.

A third major criticism is that the forces at work in our economy are rapidly driving us into one highly integrated global economy, in which the fate of all regions, towns and households will depend upon what suits the few gigantic players at the centre of the system. Even now the antics of financiers and transnational corporations in their board-rooms in Tokyo or New York can determine whether you can afford a home or whether the factory in your town closes down.

Everyone's fate is becoming increasingly dependent on decisions made by, and in the interests of, a few giant firms, many of which are now bigger than most nations. Huge regions that once prospered are no longer of any interest to them. Much of Britain is rusting away; the North-East of Brazil was dumped by international capital long ago.

Increasing numbers of people are now arguing that the only sane course of action is to strive for a high degree of economic self-sufficiency at all levels, national and regional but especially at the level of towns and suburbs. If most of the goods and services that the people in your town need can be produced by the people of the town using local resources, you are then largely immune to international economic events and the interests of transnational corporations. You will not be able to produce most things as 'efficiently' as those corporations can, but this would not matter much if people were interested in living more simply and deriving their satisfaction mostly from non-material pursuits.

AND DEVELOPMENT?

The limits to growth literature flatly contradicts the fundamental assumption underlying conventional development theory. It requires the total rejection of conceptions of development which assume indiscriminate economic growth and which take affluent Western living standards as the goal of development.

There is no chance that the world's resource and environment endowment will allow the Third World to achieve anything like our per capita resource use levels. The conclusion which has therefore been emphasised in the limits to growth literature for at least two decades is appropriately summarised by the statement: 'The rich must live more simply so that the poor may simply live.' We have to work out new systems, new values, new ways of living and new economic arrangements which will make it possible for the rich countries to live on something like their fair share of world resources. These ways have to become the goals of development for rich and poor countries alike. For the Third World the extraordinarily neglected implication is that *the goals of development have to be conceived in terms of achieving satisfactory but stable and relatively low material living standards compared with those the rich countries have now*. The concept of development must exclude any notion of affluence or endless economic growth.

It is remarkable that the literature on Third World development has given so little attention to this limits to growth theme and its crucial implications for thinking about the purpose of development. Almost all writers have plunged on taking for granted that development means striving for the affluence, industrialisation, urbanisation, and material living standards typical of the rich countries. Even the socialist or communist countries are obsessed with development conceived solely in these terms. Marxist and Dependency theories have accepted this goal as unquestioningly as conventional theories. (See Chapter 8.)

Thus two extremely profound lessons have emerged in the last twenty years. The first, from the evidence on modernisation and trickle down, is that conventional development isn't working. The second, from the limits to growth literature, is that it in any case it couldn't work.

Where does this leave us? Chapter 9 spells out the good news, which is that there is an abundant alternative.

CHAPTER 7

Maintaining Your Empire

Chapters 4 and 5 outlined the way in which the global economy functions in the interests of a few and disadvantages most people, how it gears most of the world's productive capacity to the few and delivers most of the world's wealth to them. In other words, *we who live in the rich countries have an empire*, and we could not have such high living standards if we did not have our empire.

Our empire can usefully be thought of as those regions of the world to which our corporations have access on favourable terms, enabling them to do the busiess that secures resources and cheap goods. Those corporations and their shareholders are the main beneficiaries of the empire, but consumers who live in developed countries also benefit. We obtain our coffee from the empire, for instance. If we did not have our empire, either we would not get coffee at all or we would be able to buy much less of it only at very high prices. We can have it in abundance only because large areas of Third World land which should be growing food for local people are growing coffee to export to us. We can have it only because the governments of those countries let our corporations buy their land to plant coffee, or permit and encourage their own landowners to grow coffee for export.

Our empire delivers three-quarters of the world's resource wealth to the few of us who live in rich countries.

Without our empire you could not enjoy 17 times the per capita resource use that the poorest half of the world's people have. How much oil would you get if the Western rich countries did not have access to 'our' oil-fields in the Middle East?

The Western economy could not be in such good shape if our corporations were not able to sell as much as they do to the Third World, or if they were not making relatively high profits in the Third World. About one-third of our export earnings come from the Third World. These are mainly exports of consumer goods and luxuries to Third World élite and middle class groups; they can be paid for only because Third World élites earn money from the export of coffee and tin. That money would not be available if Third World land, capital and labour were devoted to producing necessities for Third World people. Hence, the inappropriate development we promote within our empire also makes it possible for us to earn so much from exporting to Third World élites.

The most important element in the functioning of the empire is the starvation wage received by millions of people. Our coffee would cost far more if those who pick it were paid decent wages. What would coffee cost if we had to cover a wage component twenty or thirty times as big as it is now? You cannot go on enjoying living standards subsidised by low wages and repressive working conditions unless you continue to control a vast empire in which these conditions can continue to be enforced upon people who are not happy about them.

'. . . the high standard of living in the West is owing partly to the extraction of a surplus in the form of cheap labour in the LDCs.' p. 251

'Our standard of living in the West depends in part on our exploitation of cheap labour and resources in the LDCs. . . .' p. 325

W. Murdoch, *The Poverty of Nations*, Baltimore, Johns Hopkins University Press, 1980.

'But,' you may say, 'surely it is all right for us to trade; to buy things like coffee that we can't produce ourselves, so long as we pay fair prices for them. What you see as our "empire" is only the region in which we are free to trade.' This commonly held view fails to grasp the points made in Chapter 4. Though we may think we are trading and buying things at 'fair' prices, what we are in fact doing is ensuring that productive capacity that should have gone into appropriate purposes is being drawn into producing things to export at negligible benefit to most Third World people. Imperialism is not essentially a matter of theft or cheating, it is a matter of 'normal' market operations distorting development to serve the rich few, i.e., gearing the land, labour and capital within our sphere of influence primarily to our interests.

OUR RESOURCE IMPORT DEPENDENCE

Figure 5 indicates the resource dependence of the USA, a relatively resource-rich country. It went from being a net mineral exporter in 1919 to importing an estimated 20% of its mineral use in 1975.[115] By the year 2000 the US will probably be importing 80% of its mineral use.[116]

Europe is in a far worse position than the US, importing 14% of its energy use in 1952 but 59% in 1972.[117] Japan is in the most extreme position of dependence on resource imports: imports accounted for 95% of industrial materials used in the country in the mid-1970s.[118]

Overall the rich countries were importing a little under half their minerals from the Third World in the early 1970s. For the US the percentage was 42% and for Britain 61%.[119] EEC raw materials imports from the Third World average over 50% of use.[120] These proportions have been

Figure 9: US dependence on mineral imports

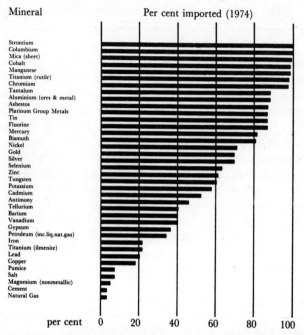

Mineral — Per cent imported (1974)

Mineral
Strontium
Columbium
Mica (sheet)
Cobalt
Manganese
Titanium (rutile)
Chromium
Tantalum
Aluminium (ores & metal)
Asbestos
Platinum Group Metals
Tin
Fluorine
Mercury
Bismuth
Nickel
Gold
Silver
Selenium
Zinc
Tungsten
Potassium
Cadmium
Antimony
Tellurium
Barium
Vanadium
Gypsum
Petroleum (inc.liq.nat.gas)
Iron
Titanium (ilmenite)
Lead
Copper
Pumice
Salt
Magnesium (nonmetallic)
Cement
Natural Gas

per cent   0   20   40   60   80   100

Adapted from N. A. Rockefeller, *Vital Resources: Reports on Energy. Food and Raw Materials*, Lexington, Lexington Books, 1977, p. 147; reprinted from *Abandon Affluence!* London, Zed Books, 1985, p. 130

increasing over time as rich countries deplete their own resources.

In addition, because our corporations are rich and technically powerful, we can simply take many things that we fancy from within the empire. Thus 90% of the $660 million worth of tuna caught off the coast of poor Pacific nations each year goes to rich countries. Those poor nations are paid $15 million in royalties, 3% of the value of the catch.[121]

Millions of hungry people live near the Pacific coast of South America, but fishing boats from the developed countries take almost all the fish caught there. Western cats could not live so well if we did not have access to these regions of our empire. The developed countries take it for granted that they should be able to collect all the sea bed resources they want, because they will be the only ones with the technical capacity to do so. But whose resources are they? Who does the world's oil and tin belong to? We do not see them as belonging to all the world's people.

At the beginning of the era of US domination, George Kennan, head of the State Department planning staff, succinctly expressed this attitude: '. . . we have about 50% of the world's wealth, but only 6.3% of its population . . . In this situation, we cannot fail to be the object of envy and resentment. Our real task in the coming period is to devise a pattern of relationships which will permit us to maintain this position of disparity without positive detriment to our national security.'[122] As Chomsky says, a central concern of US foreign policy must be ' . . . the protection of our raw materials'.[123]

Again note that in the case of access to resources cheating or trickery or illegal behaviour do not have to be resorted to. The market system makes the functioning of the imperial machine perfectly routine and 'legitimate'. It is quite in order for those with the most market power to take what they want, just by paying more for it

Benefits from the empire are not confined to material items. How orderly, civilized and safe would life in the rich countries be if there were far greater problems of scarcity? This security comes in large part because we are so affluent that there is little social conflict: Westerners do not run much risk of being trampled in a food riot.

But would the inhabitants of the Third World not be even poorer if we stopped buying their coffee? Some Third World people are indeed better off because we buy their coffee than they would be if we stopped, but that does not mean that the situation is acceptable. Third World producers are still receiving only a miniscule return for their labour or resources while others get the lion's share, and a far more appropriate arrangement can easily be imagined, for example one in which land in the Third

World could be planted with forests and gardens enabling the indigenous people to produce their own food and materials.

Although our empire is massively unjust, although it lavishes wealth on us and inflicts such savage deprivation on billions, it seems not to be driven primarily by malice, or by a desire to loot, or even by ill will. Admittedly there are many cases where there is blatant determination on the part of regimes, landlords and corporations to plunder with total indifference to the welfare of the people, but in genral most of those who operate the deadly machinery, those who invest in precisely the wrong things and who ship out the coffee, conscientiously believe they are 'helping the Third World to develop', and are therefore doing what is best for all those poor and hungry people. Such is the miracle worked by diabolically misconceived conventional development theory, which identifies as development anything that increases business turnover. That theory is the main culprit in the story, not the dictators and their hit men.

Market Violence

'Traditional fishermen of South Asia are being forced out of their occupations by mechanied trawlers which catch shrimp and other marine delicacies for the well nourished peoples of the industrial world. The indiscriminate fishing methods of the mechanised trawlers are leading to declining fish stocks, and thus to a decline in protein consumption among those who have virtually no source of protein other than fish.'
Development News Digest, 26th Dec., 1980.

'Forty thousand children die every day from malnutrition and diseases resulting from starvation. We help kill them . . . (through economic development policies which) . . . have this predictable consequence.'

> N. Chomsky, *Turning The Tide*, London, Pluto,
> 1986, p. 42.

*By far the most important and urgent goal of development
education is to help the people in the rich countries to understand
that they have an empire* – that their living standards could
not be so high if they were not taking most of the world's
wealth, much of it from poor Third World people, and that
conventional development theory constitutes the operating
manual for their imperial machine.

THE SOVIET UNION HAS AN EMPIRE TOO

The Soviet Union also maintains an empire, in which it
does many of the same nasty things that we do to control
ours. It dominates Eastern Europe and invades when it
thinks this is necessary to reassert control. More recently
it invaded Afghanistan, a Third World country. As Jenkins
and others have pointed out, to understand the way the
world works one must recognise two gigantic empires strad-
dling the globe.[124]

However, the Soviet Union's empire is quite different in
purpose and method. Theirs seems to be primarily for the
purpose of security, whereas ours is very much to do with
wealth. The Soviet Union is far more self-sufficient in
resources than the West, and it seems clear that it is not
very interested in siphoning wealth from its empire: '. . .
Soviet capital has shown little tendency to expand
abroad'.[125]

The Soviet Empire is actually a drain on Soviet wealth.
For a period after World War II the Soviet Union did
draw wealth from occupied lands, but now there is a net
flow of economic wealth from the Soviet Union to Eastern
Europe, Cuba, and the 'internal colonies' (the many
national minority groups within the Soviet Union). Cuba
costs the USSR between $4 and $6 million every day.

The USSR maintains its empire mainly as a defensive

buffer zone of territory between itself and the West. This becomes more understandable in view of its tragic military history. The USSR has been invaded and devastated a number of times; World War II alone cost the Soviet Union twenty million lives. They are very determined to make sure they are not invaded again.

The purpose of this discussion is not to support either side in the debate between capitalism and existing forms of socialism or communism: both are rejected below. However, it does seem clear that the West is open to far more serious criticism for imperial activity than the USSR. In the last three decades the West has intervened in the Third World about twelve times as often as the USSR, and has trained about ten times as many military and police personnel for Third World client regimes. Of the 120 wars that broke out between 1945 and 1976, socialist or communist countries have been involved in only six, but the rich Western countries have been involved in no few than 64.[126]

REPRESSION

Enormous effort is required to maintain the empire. It deprives hundreds of millions of people, and gears their capital, soil and labour to our interests when they would much prefer to be producing for themselves the things they need. We should not be surprised that from time to time they tend to grumble. Sometimes they may even have the temerity to protest, or demand that their wages be raised, or that some of the unused land on the plantations be made available for them to grow food. Very often they can be kept in the plantations and mines and sweatshops only by force of one kind or another. Sometimes it is economic force, which sets a choice between a miserable job in a dangerous factory or none at all. Sometimes indirect force such as censoring the press or outlawing unions is sufficient to defuse workers' demands for better pay and conditions.

Often, however, only physical violence is capable of keeping them in the mines on starvation wages.

What most people in rich countries fail to grasp is that their living standards, their empire, involves and requires extensive violence on the part of regimes which force their people to adhere to economic strategies which deprive them and enrich us. There is a direct causal connection between our high living standards and repression and terror in the Third World. The repression is usually exercised by greedy regimes anxious to crush opposition to their privileged status. It is not the rich nations who do most of the day to day work of keeping Third World masses in line: Third World governing élites do this quite willingly. Sometimes they are more heavy-handed than is necessary and the governments of the rich countries attempt to moderate their behaviour. Sometimes there is considerable conflict over human rights between rich countries and a particularly brutal 'client' regime.

The accompanying box illustrates the sorts of repressive acts taking place in many regions on a vast scale. Large numbers of people, in some countries virtually all, live in fear of violent death at the hands of their own government or its agents. Often the military and the police are the unveiled perpetrators of the violence, but at times the work is done by 'death squads' of off-duty military and police over whom the government can claim it has no control.

Repression

At midday on Tuesday 18 June 1981 a group of ten trade unionists arrived at the Presidential Palace and handed in a petition to General Pinochet. The petition, signed by hundreds of trade union leaders, called for trade union rights and freedoms, an end to arbitrary arrest and torture, and for a minimum wage. All the men were thrown into prison. Their leaders, Alamiro Guzman and Manuel Bustos, are still being

held charged with 'publishing a subversive document', and 'illegally representing workers'.
Chile Fights, 38, 1981–2, p. 7.

In Guatemala, for instance, Amnesty International estimates that there were 15,000 death squads victims in the five years between 1970 and 1975. In El Salvador, they estimate that at least 10,000 people were killed by government forces in 1980 and that summary executions as well as torture and abductions by government troops (both in and out of uniform) are increasing.
El Salvador: A Dossier, Sydney, CISCAC, 1981, p. 56.

'In Central America alone, some 60–100 civilians were being murdered by state terrorists per day in 1981, and torture was employed on a regular basis and as a "mode of governance" in more than a dozen US client states in Latin America during the 1970s.' In the early 1980s 10 to 20 Guatemalans were murdered by agents of the state every day.
   E.S. Herman, *The Real Terror Network*, Boston, South End Press, 1982.

Since June 1980 over 38,000 civilians in El Salvador have died, mostly at the hands of right-wing death squads composed of off-duty soldiers and policemen. To put that in perspective, the equivalent in Britain would be 500,000 dead – like obliterating Manchester. In addition, 650,000 Salvadoreans (out of a population of 4¼ million) are refugees. The government's campaign to suppress the guerrilla movement and its popular organizations has led to torture and misery on a scale almost unparalleled elsewhere in the world.
   The regime which presides over these 'reprehensible measures' would long since have collapsed were it not for the support of the United States – US-backed loans, in 1981 alone, amounted to $523 million.
New Internationalist, Feb., 1983, p. 30.

'For the year 1980, the Human Rights office of the Archdiocese of San Salvador tabulated 8,062 murders of "persons of the popular and progressive sectors killed for political reasons, not in military confrontations, but as a result of military operations by the Army, Security Forces and paramilitary organisations" . . .'. p. 15

'Visiting a refugee camp in Honduras, Elizabeth Hanly reports the testimony of a Salvadoran peasant woman who describes a 1983 massacre, when the National Guard came to her village in US-supplied helicopters, killing her three children among others, chopping the children to pieces and throwing them to the village pigs: "The soldiers laughed all the while," she said. Like her, other women "still had tears to cry as they told stories of sons, brothers and husbands gathered into a circle and set on fire after their legs had been broken; or of trees heavy with women hanging from their wrists, all with breasts cut off and facial skin peeled back, all slowly bleeding to death." They described how "they had worked, generations of them, all day, every day on someone else's land," their children starving or parasite-ridden. Peaceful visits to the landowners to beg for food had brought the National Guard: "We asked for food; they gave us bullets".'

N. Chomsky, *Turning the Tide*, London, Pluto, 1986.

Rich Western countries have been, to say the least, notoriously indifferent to these abuses of human rights within their own 'sphere of influence' (while rightly protesting about those in the Soviet sphere). In most cases they have made little or no effort to dissuade Third World governments from violence against their own people. But our role goes far beyond compliance. We have a long and detailed record of assisting many regimes that carry out violence on their own people. We provide them not just with economic aid, but with the arms and training they use. We literally keep many violent regimes in power. We do this under the guise of helping 'a friendly government' to 'maintain order'.

US support for the junta in El Salvador

The U.S. presence is for '. . . the maintenance of a violent and undemocratic regime . . . which, without American intervention, would clearly fall within the next three months . . .'
The Guardian, 8 March, 1981.

Many authors have extensively documented Western assistance to despicable regimes. Three deserve special mention. Klare's *Supplying Repression*[127] provides a great deal of evidence on our supply of weapons and other assistance to some of the most repressive regimes in the world. 'Between 1973 and 1978 the US gave to the ten nations with the worst repression and human rights records $1,133 million in military aid and sold them an additional $18,238 million worth of military equipment.[128]

Herman's *The Real Terror Network*[129] gives an extensively detailed account of the way in which most terrorism in the world is sponsored by the rich countries, through their assistance to their client regimes in the Third World. The title of the book is to do with the hypocritical fuss made by governments and the press in the rich countries about the terrorism inflicted by hijackers and guerrilla movements. This is terrorism on an almost trivial scale – by far the main source of terrorism is western Third World governments sponsored by rich Western countries.

Chomsky has also written a number of heavily documented works dealing with these issues. His *The Washington Connection and Third World Fascism*[130] and *Turning the Tide*[131] provide lengthy and detailed accounts of US complicity in Third World repression.

Chomsky is one of the few to stress the great default of the Western press and academics in failing to comment on the repression in which their governments are involved. He documents numerous instances of misinterpretation, or more often distortion and neglect, which have helped to reinforce widespread ignorance and misunderstanding about repression, human rights violations and terrorism in the world.[132] Chomsky and Herman and many others deal with the connection between this assistance and the conventional development model, and this link is the main concern of the remainder of this chapter.

Two other aspects of the story should briefly be mentioned. Since 1949 tens of thousands of Latin American soldiers and police have passed through US military schools such as those in Panama, where they have been taught counter-insurgency techniques and free enterprise ideology.[133] These graduates now lead the armies and many of the governments of Latin America. There are 150 such US military schools or agencies throughout the world providing training in interrogation, riot control and repression of dissent.

Assisting Repression

'. . . Washington's training has directly aided the oligarchy to carry out its terror campaigns against the peasant and worker masses. All in all US military assistance to El Salvador has strengthened the repressive military institutions that have bolstered the rule of the oligarchy.'

El Salvador: A Dossier, Sydney, CISCAC, 1981, p. 32.

Trosan and Yates list 23 countries with poor human rights records. All have been recipients of U.S. military aid. 'Without U.S. help they would be hard pressed to contain the fury of their oppressed citizens, and U.S. businesses would find it difficult to flourish. Whenever their people have rebelled and tried to, or actually did, seize power, thereby threatening foreign investments, the United States has on every occasion actively supported government repression and terror or has promoted fascist coups to overthrow popular governments.

E. Trosan and M. Yates, 'Brainwashing under freedom', *Monthly Review*, Jan., 1980, p. 44.

US aid '. . . has tended to flow disproportionately to Latin American governments which torture their citizens. . . .'

N. Chomsky, *Turning The Tide*, London, Pluto, 1986, p. 157.

'. . . the U.S. and its allies have armed the neo-fascist elites of the Third World to the teeth, and saturated them with counterinsurgency weaponry and training . . .' 'Hideous torture has become standard practice in the U.S. client fascist states.' p. 9. After documenting a number of revolting cases Chomsky states, '. . . much of the electronic and other torture gear is U.S. suppied, and great numbers of client state police and military interrogators are U.S. trained.' '. . . the U.S. is the prime sponsor of Third World fascism.' (p. 15)

N. Chomsky and E.S. Herman, *The Washington Connection and Third World Fascism*, Boston, South End Press, 1979.

Between 1950 and 1976, 3,213 Guatemalan students were trained under the U.S. military assistance programme. Between 1961 and 1973 Guatemala received 4.85 million dollars in U.S. assistance to its police force. Between 1950 and 1976 Guatemala received a total of 74.6 million dollars in U.S. military assistance. Between 1970 and 1975 161 Guatemalan military personnel received training at the U.S. Army School of the Americas, Panama Canal Zone. Between 1973 and 1976 the U.S. supplied 1,120 revolvers, 640 carbines and 160,000 cartridges to the Guatemalan National Police.

Source: Michael T. Klare, *Supplying Repression: Support for Authoritarian Regimes Abroad*, Institute for Policy Studies, Washington, 1977.

Finally, reference should be made to the 450,000 US troops stationed abroad, in a total of three hundred major military bases. The giant Subic Bay naval base in the Philippines is not there to protect American soil; it is there to protect American interests, and yours, i.e., to enable ships to patrol the sea lanes along which our wealth moves, to support client regimes, to move Rapid Deployment Forces into 'trouble spots', to remind 'subversives' what they will be up against should they try to move their country from the free enterprise way. What would happen to your living standards if all those troops were brought home? Many Third World regimes would be swept away in no time if it were not for our support. Some of them would probably be replaced by even worse communist regimes, but some would take land out of coffee and distribute it to the peasants, thus causing coffee prices to rise. Whatever else they are doing, these 450,000 troops are also protecting our high living standards.

Between 1973 and 1978 the U.S. gave to the 10 nations with the worst repression and human rights records $1,133 million in military aid (and sold them $18,238 million worth of military equipment.)

M.T. Klare, *Supplying Repression*, 1977, p. 9.

From *Abandon Affluence!*, London, Zed Books, 1985, p. 167

INTERVENTION

From time to time rich countries go beyond assisting repressive regimes and intervene either through clandestine activity or direct invasion to bring down or maintain a Third World government. The accompanying box selects a few comments from the extensive literature documenting intervention and other efforts to ensure that Third World regimes are favourable to our interests.

Propping Up (and Bringing Down) Regimes

'Our governments have intervened with troops or undercover agents to maintain friendly governments and unseat hostile ones. Since 1945 the USA intervened on average once every 18 months somewhere in the world. It included Iran 1953, Guatemala 1954, Lebanon 1958, Thailand 1959, Laos 1959, Cuba 1961, British Guiana 1963, South Vietnam 1964, Brazil 1964, Dominican Republic 1965, Cambodia 1968, Laos 1968, Chile 1973, Jamaica 1975; British intervention included Egypt 1955, Malaya 1948, Aden 1963, Brunei 1966–1978; French intervention included: French Indo-China 1946, Algeria 1956 and continuously with troops since independence in Senegal, Ivory Coast, Mauretania, Central African Republic, Chad, Zaire 1978.'
New Internationalist, October 1978, p. 5.

'In South America and Africa we continue to prop up the regimes of generals who beat their countrymen with one hand and rob them with the other.'
J. Anderson, in *The Guardian*, 20th Jan, 1980, p. 17.

'In Nicaragua, dictator Somoza has been kept in power by the brutal National Guard which operates as both an army and a policing force. The National Guard has had more U.S. training than any other military or police force in the hemisphere on a per capita basis.'

F. M. Lappe and J. Collins, *Food First*, 1977, 438.

In Haiti '. . . the richest one per cent monopolise 44% of the nation's income . . . Most of the country's land is for export crops and is owned by large landowners. Most Haitians live in misery, and the country's government is guilty of a poor human rights record. However, America supports the "Baby Doc" Duvalier dictatorship because it is anti-communist and Haiti is considered "strategic" by U.S. officials.'

Kenkelen, 1983, 'Haiti: More U.S. aid means more refugees', *Food First News*, Summer, p. 1.

The El Salvador regime '. . . has become well known for its systematic atrocities . . .' An estimated 40,000 murders have been carried out by the army in the last 8 years.

(Sydney Morning Herald, 4th Feb., 1982, p. 1.)

Training by the U.S. military '. . . has directly aided the oligarchy to carry out its terror campaigns against peasant and worker masses. . . .' 'U.S. military assistance to El Salvador has strengthened the repressive military institutions that have bolstered the rule of the oligarchy.'

El Salvador: A Dossier, Sydney, CISAC, 1981, p. 32.

'In September 1974 President Ford confirmed the fact that the Nixon administration had authorised the CIA to spend $8 million between 1970 and 1973 to weaken Allende and strengthen his opposition.'

S. Baily, *The U.S. and the Development of South America 1945–1975*, 1976, p. 206.

'Throughout the 1950s the United States government consistently fought against fundamental social and political change in underdeveloped countries. Under the guise of "protecting the world from communism" the United States has intervened in the internal affairs of at least a score of countries. In some, such as Guatemala and Iran, United States agents actually engineered the overthrow of the legitimate governments and replaced them with regimes more to American liking.'

E. Hunt and H. Sherman, *Economics*, 1972, p. 162.

Somoza Empire – Aided and Abetted by the US

The resignation of the President of Nicaragua, General Somoza, marks the end of a 46-year family dynasty that was installed and sustained and finally undermined with the help of the United States. The Somoza family owned 30% of the land that could be tilled in Nicaragua. Over the years, secured in power by unswerving loyalty to Washington, the Somoza family was able to turn Nicaragua into its personal fiefdom, growing enormously rich, while smothering all opposition in the name of fighting communism.

'Somoza empire; aided and abetted by the U.S.', *Sydney Morning Herald*, 17th July, 1979.

Many of the world's most brutal dictatorships '. . . are in place precisely because they serve U.S. interests in a joint venture with local torturers at the expense of their majorities.'

E. S. Herman, *The Real Terror Network*, Boston, South End Press, 1982, p. 15.

'. . . oligarchies would fall one by one to national revolutions if they did not get international backing.'

> J. Cockcroft, et al., *Dependence and Underdevelopment*, 1973, p. 111.

THE CONVENTIONAL DEVELOPMENT MODEL REQUIRES REPRESSION

Many parts of our empire function without repression and terror. Often it is sheer economic necessity that keeps people producing for our benefit in return for unjust wages. When it comes to getting most of the world's scarce oil supplies there is no need to burn villages – you just bid more.

But many parts of the empire cannot be run without repression and terror. Remember, the essence of the Third World problem is the unjust distribution of resources and wealth, the conventional approach to development accepts those distributions, and the many victims of the system will only comply with that approach and go on producing if they are forced to do so by physical violence or the fear of it.

Herman states the situation precisely: They '. . . will not stay quietly on the farms . . . unless they are terribly afraid . . . The economic development model favoured by the West . . . could often not be put in place without it (terror).'[134]

It is a zero-sum game. We can only have such high living standards as we do if we get most of the world's wealth, and conventional development delivers this. If most Third World people were to have satisfactory and appropriate development, most of the resources and the productive capacity now serving us would have to be devoted to their benefit instead of ours. We could not get our presently disproportionate share if it were not for repression, brutality and terror inflicted on millions of people within our empire.

The conventional approach to development deliberately maintains and enhances the privileges of the rich, because development is defined in terms of accelerating capital accumulation for investment and in terms of maximising sales, especially exports. It is an approach which intentionally deprives the poor for generations; i.e. it can only 'work' if the few with wealth retain their wealth and invest it in order to increase it as fast as possible. This approach expressly contradicts any suggestion of redistributing the existing wealth and productive capacity to those in most urgent need, and it tells the poor majority to put up with their lot at least for decades until significant trickle down arrives. Hence there is a head-on collision between development that would benefit the people and development that benefits the rich. *Conventional development deprives the people*; usually it allocates to them *some* benefit and maybe more than they would otherwise have received, but typically this is only a minute fraction of the total benefit produced and nothing like what they could be receiving had the available resources been fully devoted to appropriate development. Again, one cannot be surprised to find that at times such grotesquely unjust development strategies can only be kept in place through force and fear.

Repression is Necessary to Maintain the Empire

'To maintain its levels of production and consumption, for example, the U.S. must be assured of getting increasing amounts of the resources (because of its own decreasing reserves) or poor countries, and at a fraction of their open market value. This, in turn, requires strong American support of unpopular and dictatorial regimes which maintain political and police oppression while serving American interests, to the detriment of their own poor majorities. If, on the other hand, Third World people controlled their political economies, the export prices of their primary products would be significantly increased (as the oil producing countries are now doing). They could then use more of their resources themselves (much of the land now used to grow export cash crops – such as coffee, cocoa, bananas, tea, rubber – would be used to feed their own hungry, for example). The quantity of extracted resources could be reduced both to keep prices up and to preserve them for future use. A reduction in American consumption would also result from an independent Third World as a consequence of reduced American overseas profits, royalties, and fees.'

W. Moyer, 'De-developing the United States', in *Alternatives*, Freedom from Hunger Campaign. (From IDOC, 1973.)

'It is in the economic interest of the American corporations who have investments in these countries to maintain this social structure. It is to keep these elites in power that the United States has, through its assistance programmes, provided them with the necessary military equipment, the finance, and training.'

F. Greene, *The Enemy*, 1970.

'Whenever oppressed people have begun to struggle to better their way of life by confronting their oppressers, U.S. policy has always been on the side of the oppressor . . .'

J. Boggs, 'The kind of revolution we need', *Monthly Review*, Feb. 1986, p. 78.

'In Brazil and Greece and several other countries, very mild socialist governments . . . were overthrown by military coups supported by the CIA. In every case so far, the United States has chosen to support reactionary landlords and militarists. . . .'

W. Hunt and H. Sherman, *Economics*, 1972, 544.

'The impoverished and long abused masses of Latin America . . . will not stay quitely on the farms or

in the slums unless they are terribly afraid. As in Stroessner's Paraguay, the rich get richer only because they have the guns. The rich include a great many U.S. companies and individuals, which is why the United States has provided the guns, and much more.'
'The economic model of Third World development favoured by the West does not say "use terror", but the policies that are favoured, which would encourage foreign investment and keep wages and welfare outlays under close control, could often not be put into place without it. Privilege cannot be maintained and enlarged from already high levels if "the people" are allowed to organize, vote, and exercise any substantial power.'
'. . . the very logic of the system is to depress the masses . . . to allow unconstrained pursuit of elite benefits . . . State managers are ideologically conditioned to regard all dissent, protests and lower class organisational efforts as Communist subversion.' The support for repressive regimes is '. . . an intended outcome of US efforts to contain popular forces and preserve a favourable investment climate.' (p. 126)
These policies of repression are '. . . designed to keep large numbers in a state of serious deprivation while small upper classes, multinational business interests and elites of military enforcers "develop" these countries without any democratic constraint.'

E. S. Herman, *The Real Terror Network*, Boston, South End Press, 1982

'The basic fact is that the United States has organized under its sponsorship and protection a neo-colonial system of client states ruled mainly by terror and serving the interests of a small local and foreign business and military elite.'
'U.S. economic interests in the Third World have dictated a policy of containing revolution, preserving an open door for U.S. investment, and assuring

favourable conditions of investment. Reformist efforts to improve the lot of the poor and oppressed, including the encouragement of independent trade unions, are not conducive to a favourable climate of investment.'

'In order to impose the model of development which gives privilege to small minorities, it was necessary to create or maintain a repressive State. The development they wish to impose on the country can only provoke indignation among the people ... If there were any type of freedom left the cries of protest would be so great that the only solution has been to impose absolute silence.'

> N. Chomsky and E. S. Herman, *The Washington Connection and Third World Fascism*, Boston, South End Press, 1979.

'WOULDN'T THEY SELL TO US ANYWAY?'

A view which is commonly encountered runs: 'But we don't need arms and violence to secure resources. We don't have to maintain an empire. Even if a Third World country turned communist it would still eagerly sell its resources to us.' Of course poor countries, even poor socialist or communist countries, are eager to sell their resources to us. Even countries like Nicaragua or Cuba whose governments are more willing to devote export earnings to appropriate development, must compete in the global market place to sell their produce. If a poor socialist tin exporting country were to demand much higher prices so that its tin miners could be paid decent wages and have improved working conditions, we would simply ignore that country and buy from some other country prepared to sell at the lowest possible price, and see its miners continue to die from mine dust, malnutrition, and avoidable accidents.[135]

They would continue to sell to us, and at current prices, *so long as no alternative was possible*. But the danger for us is that if many countries opted out of our sphere of influence other alternatives would become conceivable, such as South-South trading blocs, or more effective links with the Eastern bloc, or boycotts of the West.

There is a far more important issue here. *No socialist or communist government giving top priority to the needs of its people would, if it had any choice in the matter, willingly sell natural resources, especially the produce of its soils, at such very low returns to the common people as the typical Third World government does now.*

As we have seen, the essential evil within the present system is to do with the extremely uneven shares of wealth received. For instance, the bulk of the wealth generated by coffee production now goes to plantation owners, trans-national corporations, and consumers in rich countries. Coffee pickers often receive less than 1% of the retail value of the coffee they pick. *Any genuinely socialist government would drastically redistribute those shares,* or convert the land to food production, if it could, meaning that people in rich countries would then get far less coffee etc., or pay much higher prices. Hence we again arrive at the basic conclusion: a more just deal cannot be given to the people in the Third World unless rich countries accept a marked reduction in the share they receive from wealth generated in the Third World.

Any genuinely socialist government would certainly clamp down on the bonanza terms now granted to trans-national corporations, such as tax-free periods of up to twenty years, few restrictions on transfers of funds, repressive labour laws, low safety standards, controlled or banned unions, and weak environmental laws. These conditions are among the mechanisms whereby wealth is transferred. When a hungry labourer picks coffee for you at one-twentieth the wage you would expect, you and the coffee corporation are enriched at his expense, and he will not go on picking your coffee unless he is forced to do so by economic circumstances or fear of violence.

> '. . . no democratic government could permit its country's resources to be developed on terms favourable to American corporate and government interests.'
> I. Katznelson and M. Kesselman, *The Politics of Power*, 1983, p. 234.

CRUSHING ALTERNATIVE EXAMPLES

A great deal of effort goes into ensuring that alternative, non-capitalist approaches to development do not succeed. If any of them were to succeed, they might become examples showing other Third World countries that it was possible and desirable to pursue an appropriate path to development. This explains why even the smallest countries that opt for a non-capitalist path can become the object of intense economic and military violence. If a tiny Nicaragua or Grenada can opt out of the capitalist path to development and succeed through an alternative approach, then this would show larger countries that they could more easily do the same.

> '. . . the tinier and weaker the country, the less endowed it is with resources, the more dangerous it is. If even a marginal and impoverished country can begin to utilize its own limited human and material resources and can undertake programs of development geared to the needs of the domestic population, then others may ask: why not us?'
> N. Chomsky, *Turning the Tide*, London, Pluto, 1986, p. 72.

Hence the US has waged war on Nicaragua as intensely as international opinion has permitted. Nicaragua is one of the most pathetically weak and impoverished countries in the world, due primarily to forty years of dictatorship and exploitation at the hands of Somosa, installed by the US and constantly propped up by US aid and arms. US military aid between 1950 and 1975 totalled $25.5 million.

Somoza exemplified brutal rule in the interests of a greedy local élite, while making his country a paradise for foreign investors. At the end of his rule his family owned approximately one-third of the country's arable land. Over 25,000 people were killed '. . . in the 41 year reign of terror aided and abetted by Washington. . . .'[136] Against all odds the Sandinistas finally overthrew Somoza. Despite great difficulties and many admitted mistakes they have achieved rapid improvements in the living conditions of most people, putting to shame almost all other countries in the region with the exception of Cuba. The USA has consistently done all it could to destroy the experiment. In the mid-1980s the US was spending millions of dollars in aid to the Contras fighting against the Sandinista government, and direct US invasion seemed imminent. In addition, all possible strategies for economic sabotage were being exercised, such as blocking trade, loans and aid, and attempting to have allies do likewise.

What about the cliam that Nicaragua is a communist country right on America's doorstep? In terms of the proportion of its economy in private hands – over 60% – Nicaragua is less socialist or communist than Australia.

The revolution was made by popular resistance, and the communist party was not centrally involved in it.[137] There are few communists within high government circles, but they are far from dominant.[138] Despite many claims, the USA has not been able to give any impressive evidence that Nicaragua is a base for Russian or Cuban activity, or is supplying arms to guerrillas in other regions such as El Salvador. As Berryman emphasises, '. . . at no point has the Reagan administration furnished convincing public proof for its repeated assertions that Nicaragua has sent massive and continual arms shipments to the Salvadoran rebels.'[139]

Nicaragua's unforgivable error has been to reject development defined in terms of permitting foreign investors, market forces, the profit motive and the obsession with sheer growth to determine what happens, and to insist on some degree of rational control and planning of development in the interests of the majority. The US onslaught is intended to make sure that such an alternative path is not seen to succeed in Nicaragua.[140]

Chomsky points out how this general policy was well served by the large scale bombing and poisoning of Vietnam. More bombs were dropped there than all sides dropped in World War II, and huge quantities of defoliants were sprayed on forests and other ecosystems, making Vietnam's chances of satisfactory economic progress after the war very difficult.

If a country does succeed in breaking away from the capitalist approach to development, you can be fairly certain that it will then be driven into the communist sphere, which then justifies past and future attacks – 'See, we told you they were communist all along.'[141] Cuba had almost no contact with the USSR until *eighteen months after* completing its revolution. The economic blockade imposed by the US was the main factor leading Cuba to approach the USSR.[142] Any country that successfully rebels will find itself cut off from loans, investment or trade with the US and as many US allies as possible. In addition to this attempt to destabilise the economy, the US will undoubtedly underwrite whatever subversion it can, via the CIA if not via direct military confrontation. In the face of these hindrances and attacks, the only place where the rebel country is likely to find the economic or military assistance necessary for survival will be the Soviet sphere. The Russians usually grant assistance when asked by anti-Western governments, but not always. Allende's Chile was a remarkable case of indifference on the part of the USSR.[143]

THE USES OF THE COLD WAR

Chomsky is also one of many who explains how the cold war between Russia and the USA is in large part due to the usefulness of the 'Russian Threat' to US administrations which have the problem of justifying to the American people the intervention and repression they are involved in within the Third World. It is most convenient to be able to say: 'We are only invading to put down communist subversion inspired and armed by Russia as part of its ceaseless quest to convert the world to communism.' Without this screen the American public would be much more likely to object to maintaining an undesirable regime that will allow American corporations to do business on very favourable terms.

There is a considerable literature explaining the origins and maintenance of the Cold War in these terms.[144] Its central argument is that to a large extent the post World War II era of hostility between the USSR and the USA was initiated by the US administration as a device to ensure otherwise uncertain domestic support for the new role which the administration wanted America to play in the world. At the end of World War II the US suddenly found itself to be by far the most powerful nation on the world stage, in a position to expand international business activity rapidly and to exercise unquestioned political domination. Its economy had been cured from the lingering depression and had been primed by war production. The US had suffered no war damage, while all possible rivals in Europe lay in ruins. But there was a strong isolationist sentiment within America: many people had wanted America to keep out of global affairs and concentrate on building a more independent and autonomous America, basing economic prosperity on the large internal market rather than on trade and foreign investment.

These forces were a major obstacle to those in government at the end of World War II who wanted America to grasp the opportunity to expand business activity throughout the world. These officials had considerable difficulty in getting public support for measures designed to assist European recovery, such as the substantial loan made to Britain and the Marshall aid plan.

> 'Governments cannot export revolution.'
> G. Blasier, *The Giant's Rival*, 1983, p. 153.

Although there is considerable debate about the origins of the Cold War, it is plausible that stirring up fear of the Russians was an important factor. Certainly it was then and it has since been a very useful device for enlisting public opinion in support of various foreign and domestic policies. A number of books have been written explaining the many uses that various interest groups have made of the 'Russian Threat Thesis'[145] (while debunking the thesis itself).

These issues lead to the conclusion that although there are other factors involved, and although American behaviour may also be driven by some admirable motives, US Foreign policy is *essentially about keeping as much of the world as possible open to the operations of American corporations, and keeping it to the free enterprise way* – all of which enables the rich countries to secure most of the world's wealth.

> '. . . the basic intent of U.S. foreign policy has been to facilitate the overseas expansion of U.S. business'.
> F. Block, *The Origins of International Economic Disorder*, 1977, p. 193.

'COMMUNIST SUBVERSION'

Whenever the US or another Western country intervenes in the Third World or assists a brutal Third World regime to harass or kill more of its own people, we always say: 'But we are only helping a friendly government to protect itself against communist subversion'. This is the central issue for anyone who wishes to come to terms with violence in the Third World. The conventional position admits that a number of the governments we support are far from satisfactory in their respect for human rights, but argues that we have to support them in order to prevent communist takeover. The Reagan administration has clearly stated on a number of occasions that all the turmoil in Central America is due to subversion by the Russians: as Reagan himself has said, 'The troubles in Central America are a power play by Cuba and the Soviet Union, pure and simple.'[146]

However, this whole argument constitutes one of the most easily dismissed myths surrounding US foreign policy. *The pressue for revolution in the Third World derives from conditions which cry out for revolution, not from Russian subversion.*

Firstly, the historical record shows that communists have been quite unimportant in revolutionary movements in Latin America. In fact they have often been embarrassed at not being given much of a part to play by those who have organised revolutions. As Berryman says, '. . . the guerilla movements in Guatemala, Nicaragua, and El Salvador . . . were not led by communist parties, i.e., parties linked to Moscow. In fact the existing communist parties in those countries repeatedly denounced the guerilla organisations as "adventurist".'[147] Blasier also documents this point, stressing that communist parties have had only minor roles at best in these movements.[148] He documents how the Cuban revolution was a people's revolt against a regime supported for years by the USA, in which the issue of communism was almost irrelevant. 'Cuban communists and the U.S.S.R. contributed little or nothing . . .'[149] Castro was in conflict with the local communists and later used their party to his advantage.[150] 'The communist parties in Latin America are being forced to come to terms with the reality that such broad, loose, national fronts are

We are going to develop!
We'll build TV factories
We will plant more coffee.
We'll build tourist hotels.

But we are hungry.
Can't we produce
more food for us
first?

What, distort market forces? Interfere with
free enterprise?? Scare off foreign investment?!
COMMUNIST SUBVERSIVE!!!

From *Abandon Affluence!*, London, Zed., 1985, p. 174

leading and winning revolutions almost without them.'[151]
Blasier adds, 'In Central America, the revolutionary
parties are led by non-communists . . . communists in Latin
America have never led a revolution.'[152]

Secondly, despite a great deal of effort the US administration has been spectacularly unable to come up with
evidence of Russian assistance to guerrilla movements in
Latin America. The most glaring failure has been their
claim that Nicaragua has supplied arms in El Salvador.[153]

In most cases revolutionary movements (as distinct from anti-Western governments) have received little or no military assistance from Russia or Cuba.[154] Mostly they have to arm themselves, usually from captured weapons. The USSR's record of assistance for revolutionary movements is surprisingly uneven. On a number of occasions they have given little or no support, notably to Allende in Chile. Cases such as these seem to reveal the Soviet Union to be about as self-interested as most countries are. Often it has realised that to become entangled in foreign revolutions would be to cause itself more problems than it is worth.

The fact that the USSR sometimes does give arms and other assistance to revolutionary movements is not very significant in this discussion. Such assistance cannot be the cause of the trouble. If you can see that a situation has festered to the stage where a revolutionary movement has struggled into existence and is seeking arms, then you know that there are serious problems of justice and repression which should have been attended to long ago. Sometimes it would be an indisputably good thing if the Russians or Cubans were providing the arms which are the only hope that revolutionary movements have of liberating themselves from the greedy and blood-thirsty regimes the West is supporting.

Most importantly, *revolutions can only be made by oppressed people*. Anyone who has the slightest understanding of social movements in general and revolution in particular realises how extremely difficult it is to get a revolution going. It is absurd for the Reagan administration to suggest that Russian or Cuban agents could come into a Central American country and stir up a revolution. It is amazing what oppressed, exploited and brutalised people will continue to endure without attempting to hit back. In much of Latin America people have put up with decades, even centuries, of the most appalling treatment from exploitative and vicious ruling classes, without mounting any significant threat to those regimes. Many attempts to initiate revolution among people who have the most clear-cut reasons for hitting back have failed to win significant support from the oppressed classes. If there is any move whatsoever towards popular rebellion, let alone a successful people's revolution, you can be sure that there has been a long history of enormous suffering at the hands of a brutal and predatory ruling class. As Blasier says: 'American leaders have not understood the fundamental causes of the revolutions . . . Their most serious misperception has been that the U.S.S.R., acting throughout the Communist parties or conspiratorial activities, actually caused social revolution in Latin America.'[155] Chomsky and many others would argue that American leaders understand the situation only too well. The weakness in Blasier's account is its failure to recognise that these and other aspects of US foreign policy are not mistakes, but deliberate and essential elements in the defence of the empire.

It is possible for subversive agents to enter a Third World country and organise a coup without involving the people in general. The USA and the USSR have often been involved in activities of this sort. But this is entirely different from a popular revolt.

The groups making most mileage out of 'the communist threat' are the ruling classes of the Third World, especially in Latin America. At the slightest hint of a call for social justice or change that might impinge upon their interests they immediately cry 'communism'. Dissent of any kind is branded as communist subversion. This has been a marvellous mechanism for destroying challenges to their privileges, especially as it usually guarantees US support. Herman sums the situation up neatly: 'Among Latin American elites, a peasant asking for a higher wage or a priest helping organise a peasant cooperative is a communist. And someone going so far as to suggest land reform or a more equitable tax system is a communist fanatic'. Hence '. . . peasants trying to improve themselves, priests with the slightest humanistic proclivities, and naturally anyone seriously challenging the status quo, are communist . . .

evil, a threat to "security", and must be treated accordingly.'[156]

Any Dissent is Communist Subversion

The military juntas adopt a free enterprise – blind growth model. '. . . Since free enterprise-growth-profits-USA are good, anybody challenging these concepts of their consequences is ipso facto a Communist-subversive-enemy.' Hence '. . . any resistance to business power and privilege in the interests of equity . . . is a National Security and police problem . . . From the standpoint of the multinationals and latifundists, this is superb doctrine: reform is equated with subversion. In the words of the Guatemalan Foreign Minister, Toriello, any Latin American government that exerts itself to bring about a truly national program which affects the interests of the powerful foreign companies, in whose hands the wealth and the basic resources in large part repose in Latin America, will be pointed out as Communist . . . and so will be threatened with foreign intervention.'

N. Chomsky, *Turning the Tide*, London, Pluto, 1986.

THEIR TERRORISM MAKES SENSE

If the foregoing account of the situation is more or less valid it becomes understandable why some Third World rebel groups resort to hijacking, kidnapping and terrorist bombing. It is not surprising that some of them finally try to hit back with apparently indiscriminate violence. Our media always react with horror and disbelief. They regard these acts as outrageously unjustified, indeed unintelligible, and they portray the hijackers and bomb planters as fanatical, irrational monsters.

Are you sure that if you had been hungry and disease-ridden all your life, had been obliged to sell one of your children to have sufficient money to save the others from perishing, had cut a tonne of sugar cane a day for starvation wages or worked seven days a week for thirteen years in mine dust that killed your father when you yourself were dying from silicosis and TB[157], that *you* would not want to hit out? If you knew that your miserable conditions made possible the opulent waste enjoyed by the pampered few who can afford to fly in jumbo jets, and could see that the rich countries devoted millons of dollars every year to maintaining the empire, enriching them and depriving you, are you quite sure that you would not react violently?

Their terrorism is quite understandable; yet in my view it is seriously mistaken. Sometimes in war situations terror can make sense as a tactic, for instance to prevent peasants from giving assistance to the other side. But hijacking and bombing intended to hit civilians in the rich countries would seem to be incapable of contributing to what has to be done. The vast changes necessary in global economic structures will not be possible until we have first achieved widespread change in the world views and values of the people of both rich and poor countries. The only way this can be done is through decades of patient educational effort.

THE WORLD SYSTEMS PERSPECTIVE

Having been the dominant world power since World War II, the USA deserves condemnation for being by far the most significant agent of repression, interference and inappropriate development in the Third World. If you wish, heap as much contempt on the USSR for its imperial behaviour, but it is necessary to see all this in the context of the four-hundred-year history of the current world economic system. Wallerstein and the school of thought known as World Systems Theory argue that many aspects of our situation are best approached in terms of a world economic system which came into existence for the first time several hundred years ago – the capitalist system.[158] Before then there were many independent economic systems rather than one integrated global system. These systems were not driven by the incredibly powerful force which has since come to shape our world – the drive to accumulate. Capitalism is about investing to make as much profit as possible, in an endless spiral of capital accumulation. This mentality was not dominant in the feudal era. The very few people who were then concerned about accumulating wealth were often more or less despised. What was of overwhelming importance to most people was not becoming richer, nor even material progress and rising living standards, but the salvation of their souls. The relatively sudden coming of the capitalist spirit plunged the world into an accelerating whirlpool of change, 'progress', and imperial expansion.

World Systems Theory argues that to make most sense of the last three or four centuries it is necessary to focus on the struggle for control of the world capitalist system, and the sequence of dominant powers this has brought about. Each has strutted the stage for a period, enforcing rules which suited itself and grabbing most of the available booty. The Portuguese were displaced by the Spanish, then the Dutch were top dog for a time. Britain had the longest reign, fighting off challenges from France and Germany. After World War II the USA burst through to unrivalled 'leadership'.

But the 'American century' lasted a mere 25 years; by the late 1960s the USA was fading. Now it is in serious economic difficulties, with low and falling rates of productivity, profits and investment, a chronically adverse balance of trade, and a series of record-breaking budget deficits which have made it by far the world's most indebted nation.

The next power to dominate the world capitalist system will be Japan. Largely because of its spectacular trading success, Japan is presently embarrassed by the volume of capital it has accumulated, little of which can be used to import so it is increasingly being invested in the Third World.

The World Systems perspective helps us to see history as a ceaseless imperial quest. A glance at the literature on international relations reinforces this image. Nations are about the largely amoral pursuit of greater wealth, power and prestige. A number of studies conclude that this must be the basic frame for understanding war in the modern era.[159] The drive to expand national wealth, power and prestige has a very strong tendency to lead nations into violent conflict. Sometimes peace can be maintained by the domination of one power which is able to force all others to keep to the order it prefers, or by shaky balance of power alliances. The most dangerous period seems to be when a rising challenger threatens to surpass the reigning power. Many specific conflicts are understandable in terms of expansion and challenges to domination of an empire. Japan's entry into World War II, for example, was significantly motivated by desire for greater access to resources.

Of course Britain was not an aggressor in World War I or II – because it had previously grabbed all the available loot and held off counterclaims through 72 colonial wars! Those two World Wars were largely about powers which had previously been squeezed out by Britain demanding more of the global pickings.

Extremely important implications for the question of long term global peace and development come from this general World Systems perspective. We cannot expect to achieve a peaceful world, nor can we expect to see satisfactory development, until we grow out of this greedy and infantile imperial mentality. If nations continue to insist on clawing their way over each other to ever greater wealth, power and prestige, then we will continue to have an infallible recipe for endless and accelerating domination, conflict and imperialism. Chapter 6 showed that the richest nations are far past the point where they can be so affluent and powerful and prestigious without dominating other nations and running an empire from which the required wealth is to be accumulated. The USA just happens to be the current top dog. It is no more contemptible than the rest; if New Zealand or Ireland were able to dominate the world system it would surely do so, given that most people in any country subscribe to the false ideas that drive imperialism, especially belief in endlessly rising 'living standards' and GNP.

We cannot expect to see an end to imperialism and the domination of nations, nor to international conflict, until we outgrow our mindless obsession with affluence, growth and power.

CONCLUSIONS

Much of the preceding account has been put in terms which blame the Third World problem on 'us', the people who live in rich countries. It must be emphasised that some of us are far more culpable than others. By far the greatest beneficiaries of the unjust global economy are the managers and shareholders of the transnational corporations and financial institutions, the 5% of people in the rich countries who own and control half of all wealth, and almost all of the invested capital.[160] Marxist theory, however, is all too ready to absolve the rest of us from responsibility. Admittedly we are obliged to work at purposes set by capitalists, and our world views and values are largely shaped by them through their ownership of the means of production and the media. It is to a large extent they who have moulded us into ravenous consumer lifestyles. But the rest of us are willing beneficiaries. We happily buy the coffee the transnational corporations deliver, and we eagerly use up our four-fifths of the world's resource output. We are a large and necessary part of the problem and, more importantly, we could break out at any moment if we chose to. We could refuse the consumer way if we took seriously the appropriate ideas, values and commitments. There are powerful forces working against it, but at some point questions of personal responsibility begin.

The overridingly important implication of the last three chapters is that satisfactory development is totally inconceivable unless and until we make a fundamental change from an economic system in which the basic characteristics are production for profit, freedom for capital, market forces, and endless and indiscriminate growth. The great significance of the short history of development is that it has shown how an economic system driven by these factors results in development only in the interests of the rich participants, how it results in the grotesque maldistribution of available wealth and productive capacity, and how it results in obscenely inappropriate development in view of the needs of most people. For a time it could be argued that although the rich were getting most of the benefit, there would be enough trickle down to solve the problems of the majority in an acceptable time span. We now have overwhelmingly strong grounds for rejecting any such claim.

The fundamentally important conclusion is that the most direct cause of Third World problems is commitment to the market system and to the growth economy. There are many other causes. The Third World does have a serious population problem, it has difficult climates, it lacks expertise, and many of its governments are farcically incompetent and corrupt. But by far the greatest problem is the maldistribution of existing resources, wealth and productive capacity, both between nations and within individual Third World countries. Again it should be said that while the basically free enterprise or capitalist approach to development is disastrous, this does not mean that the typical big-state socialist or communist way is the answer. Chapter 9 will argue for a third alternative.

CHAPTER 8

Clarifying Radical Development Theory

This chapter steps aside from the main argument of the book in order to apply its concepts to some key themes in the current discussion of development theory. The literature on development theory is large, complicated and controversial; there are many unsettled arguments and disputes, especially within the radical camp, and it is not easy even for professional students of the scene to work out a coherent position.

THE BRIEF BUT CHAOTIC HISTORY OF DEVELOPMENT THEORY

It is important to recognise that although some people were writing about what we now call 'underdeveloped countries' last century, development theory really only started after World War II, and the present huge volume of literature has built up mostly since the early 1960s. For the first two decades the modernisation view was generally taken as being correct, almost without challenge. By the 1970s, however, Dependency theory had burst onto the stage, strenuously rejecting the basic assumptions of modernisation. For a time Dependency theory seemed to have been generally accepted by the rapidly increasing numbers of theorists critical of modernisation theory, but its reign was short lived. Although built from a more or less Marxist perspective, Dependency theory departed from it on some key points, and before long some of the most heated debates took the form of orthodox Marxist attacks upon Dependency. Explicit analyses in modernisation terms, let alone attempts to defend that perspective, are now scarce indeed in the academic literature (though unfortunately they still abound in the textbooks).[161]

The situation in the mid-1980s is chaotic and unsatisfactory. A number of important but obscure and at times confused debates are going on. It seems to have taken an extraordinary quantity of paper and ink to achieve very little progress, due in large part to the refusal of most participants to express themselves succinctly, or even to define terms, notably 'dependence'. How much time and energy has it taken just to establish the inadequacy of Dependency theory? Has *any* progress been made towards the emergence of a sound alternative to Dependency as a basis for critical theorising?

A number of authors have expressed regret at the depressing state of the critical development literature. As Howe says, 'The theory of imperialism is in profound disarray.'[162] It is most unfortunate that in a period when the evidence has so clearly revealed conventional theory to be inadequate, critical development theorists have not been able to come forward with a clear, simple, agreed and convincing explanation of why satisfactory development is not occurring, nor firm implications for alternative strategies.[163]

DEPENDENCY THEORY

Dependency theory suddenly emerged as a much needed challenge to the relatively long and quiet reign of modernisation theory. The writings of A. G. Frank in particular helped to make Dependency the orthodox position among critical theorists.

The key elements in Dependency theory were the claims that:

– the Third World is not developing towards 'take-off' to self sufficient economic growth, but is stagnating;
– the process of development under capitalism only involves development for the 'core' or rich countries, while the Third World or 'peripheral' countries are 'under-developed'; thus underdevelopment is a state that is created in the 'peripheral' countries by capitalist development in the 'core' countries;
– this condition is characterised primarily by dependence on the rich countries;
– the lack of development in the Third World is essentially due to the loss of capital drained out to the core countries;
– analysis should focus on relations between rich and poor nations, on international flows of wealth and the effects of trade, rather than on class relations or modes of production.

Although Dependency theory took off in more or less the right direction after modernisation, and made a valuable contribution to the rise of critical development thinking, a number of serious objections emerged, and by the late 1970s critical theorists in general seemed to have abandoned this position.

Firstly, dependence does not seem to be the key problem underlying Third World underdevelopment. A high degree of economic dependence has not stopped Canada or Australia or the Newly Industrialising Countries from developing.

Nor does the stagnation thesis seem to be satisfactory. Essential to Dependency theory is the argument that contact with the rich countries has blocked Third World development and has led to stagnation and underdevelopment. This seems to be a valid and important comment on the history of some countries, especially in Latin America, but as a generalisation about what is currently happening in development it has recently been the main point of attack on Dependency theory.[164] Not only have the NICs made spectacular growth, but according to World Bank

figures the LDCs as a whole have grown faster than the
rich countries over recent years.[165] This issue has been a
major point of division between Dependency and Marxist
theorists.[166]

The term introduced in Chapter 3 seem to permit a
better representation of the situation than either of these
theories. Although virtual stagnation has been the experience of large numbers of Third World *people*, in GNP terms
considerable development has clearly taken place in just
about all Third World *countries*, and quite rapid development has occurred in many. The important point is that
it has often been highly inappropriate development.

It is worth noting that by casting the problem of development in terms of stagnation or underdevelopment, Dependency theory reveals the same fundamental assumption
that conventional theory builds on. Both take development
to be unidimensional, assuming that it is only about
increasing the amount of indiscriminate business turnover
and capital accumulation, with no questions asked about
the appropriateness of development nor the possibility that
highly satisfactory development might be possible without
much economic growth.[167] Possibly an even more important
criticism is that the emphasis on dependence and the domi-
nance of the core countries in the world economy has had
the unfortunate effect of reinforcing the belief that Third
World people cannot do anything to improve their own
situation, when it will be argued in Chapter 9 that there is
considerable scope for even the poorest people to undertake
appropriate development strategies.

LOSS OF CAPITAL?

Dependency theory argues that the reason for the underdeveloped and stagnant state of the Third World is that
its surplus wealth is drained out to rich countries. There
are long-standing and very unsettled debates about the
significance of capital flows for underdevelopment and
colonialism. Firstly, is there a significant loss? Some

authors have argued that there is not. Mack and Leaver (1981), for example, conclude that the net outflow is only about 1.2% of Third World GNP, much too small either to explain the underdevelopment of the Third World, or to support the Marxist claim that foreign investment and imperialism are necessary for the health of mature capitalism.

It is likely that if we had good information on the magnitude of transfer pricing arrangements used by transnational corporations on shipments between their subsidiaries, much more substantial losses would be revealed. According to Harrison, profit repatriation concealed by transfer pricing could amount to $90 billion p.a. 15 times the declared profit repatriation.[168] In addition, repayments on loans to first world banks have exceeded new loans by around $30 billion p.a. in some years during the early 1980s, but this is only a recent phenomenon. The point is that there probably has been a considerable loss of capital from the Third World throughout the last few decades, but in the absence of clear figures this cannot be used as a sound foundation for pronouncements on what is wrong about development.

This sort of international balance sheet can never reveal one of the most obviously unacceptable and unjust processes occurring – the hugh quantities of 'wealth' flowing from poor plantation workers to rich consumers in the first world through the payment of extremely low wages. Those workers create wealth which enriches us, but they themselves receive a minute proportion of the wealth they create. Nor can such a balance sheet reveal the unjust transfer that occurs when fishing boats from the rich nations take fish from waters around poor and hungry nations, or pay low royalties, or destroy ecological capital (notably forests) that will mean increased problems and costs for the poor country in later years.

But these unsettled issues can be avoided: loss of capital cannot be the essential problem underlying underdevelopment, *because the Third World lacks neither capital nor develop-*

ment. A great deal of development is very obviously taking place. More importantly, over 85% of the capital invested in the Third World by foreign investors is raised in the Third World, meaning that there is plenty of capital there, especially in view of the relatively small amounts which appropriate development would require. The problem is not insufficient development or capital, but that the quite adequate quantities of capital and other resources are grossly unevenly distributed (for instance, 3% of Third World landowners hold 80% of Third World land), and that these resources are put largely into inappropriate sorts of developments. Nor need we become entangled in the Marxist argument that mature capitalism requires foreign investment and imperialism; maybe it does, but this is far from clearly established and therefore does not constitute a satisfactory foundation from which we can argue about what is wrong and what ought to be done.

TERMS OF TRADE?

One branch of the Dependency school argued that the Third World's problems are essentially due to the loss of surplus resulting from falls in the prices which their exports receive and the rises in the prices of their imports from the rich world. Impressive figures can be quoted, but these tend to be selected from periods of time or regions which suit the argument. The long term evidence seems to show little or no significant deterioration in the Third World's terms of trade. As was argued in Chapter 5, the trade arena reveals a number of disturbing things about the Third World's treatment, but focusing on trade alone does not get us to the heart of the development problem.

What difference would be made if we vastly improved the Third World's terms of trade by suddenly agreeing to pay twice as much for our imports? Third World exporters (many of them transnationals from the rich world) would become far richer, governments would collect a little more tax, and spend it on more power stations and dams – while the workers in the export plantations went on being paid the lowest possible wages and the poor majority of people went on watching the development of things of no benefit to them. The poor might in time gain some trickle down benefits, but their main problem is that they receive very little of the wealth *received in the Third World* from the export of the goods they produce, the wrong things are produced with the additional income, and the wrong industries are set up. Changing trade arrangements would not make much difference to these effects.

MARXIST THEORY STRIKES BACK

Since the early 1970s Marxists have attempted to regain the lead from Dependency theory in explaining development. Bill Warren's contributions have become well known as efforts to refute the Dependency stagnation thesis.[169] Marx argued that there was one normal sequence of capitalist development, and it would culminate in revolution and socialism. Contact with rich capitalist countries would start to move a Third World country down that path (an analysis which is remarkably similar to Rostow's stage theory). However, Lenin, Baran, Baran and Sweezy, Frank, and Dependency theory in general, broke with this tradition and argued that capitalist development in the rich world blocks normal capitalist development in the Third World.[170] As Frank said, it 'underdevelops' poor countries and results in stagnation. This has come to be referred to as the 'neo-Marxist' position. Warren has been influential in claiming that the Third World is not stagnating and is actually making normal capitalist development. He and orthodox Marxists are delighted about this, because they see it as moving the Third World towards what is to them the only real solution, the revolutionary overthrow of capitalism.

Other more recent Marxist contributions have advanced our understanding of various aspects of development, especially concerning the historical emergence of capitalism and its spread into the Third World throughout the previous centuries. Brenner, for example, offers an impressive argument for the importance of Marxist theory in these realms.[171]

THE ARTICULATION OF MODES OF PRODUCTION

One of Frank's influential claims was that modernisation theory has been mistaken in seeing most of the Third World as having a feudal social order thwarting the advance of the modern or capitalist sector. Frank argued that these economies must be understood as capitalist, and that the stagnant and oppressive relations evident on the plantation were just aspects of the underdevelopment in the periphery created by capitalist development for the benefit of the core.

This thesis has provoked a literature now identified by some as putting forward a distinct theoretical position concerned with analysing the different 'modes of production' existing in the Third World, and the various ways in which these are combined (articulated) in different regions and under different social conditions. The production of coffee, for example, probably involves some purely capitalist elements at the level of manufacture, finance and shipping, with a variety of pre-capitalist relations, perhaps feudal or even slave relations, between plantation owners and workers. The particular arrangement in Brazil probably differs from that in Colombia. The exploration of these issues is another tribute to the value of Marx's theory and its emphasis on analysing in terms of modes of production.

PROBLEMS FOR THE MORALISER

The trouble with much of this recent theorising, especially from the Marxist camp, is that it does not facilitate moralising! Anyone who wants to complain about what is wrong with the world and what needs to be changed will not find much help in the voluminous literature on the historical emergence of capitalism, or on modes of production, or on Warren's claims. According to Marx, what is essentially wrong is the capitalist mode of production, because it involves capitalist employers exploiting workers. This, however, is not a very helpful base from which to offer explanations as to what is wrong *about development*, to explain the relations between rich and poor countries and the way in which the global economy distributes things, or to offer statements about what might constitute satisfactory development. The argument in Chapter 3 was that the concepts introduced there provide a better foundation for the important task of complaining about the current state of affairs and pointing to alternative strategies.

THE INSUFFICIENCY OF MARXIST THEORY FOR UNDERSTANDING AND EVALUATING THE STATE OF DEVELOPMENT

Marxist theory is by far the most valuable theoretical base for understanding our social world, its chaotic history, its enormous problems and its uncertain prospect. My *Abandon Affluence!*[172] is a detailed analysis of our global situation largely in terms of the concepts, arguments and insights that Marx provided for us. I now want to argue, however, that when it comes to understanding what is wrong about development and why, and the nature of satisfactory or appropriate development, Marxist theory is far from sufficient, and indeed quite misleading. Some of Marx's concepts are crucial for the task, but one must go well beyond them. In fact one must focus on concepts which Marx explicitly rejected, and on concepts which Marx totally failed to recognise.

The chief concern in this book has been with a perspective which facilitates the *evaluation* of development, rich world/poor world relations, and the way the global economy works. Its main concern is not with understanding the historical origins and development of capitalism or its spread through the Third World, purposes for which Marxist theory is unrivalled.

Marxists insist that the essence of capitalism is its mode of production. This involves free labour being exploited by capital – workers who are free of ties, such as to guilds or feudal lords, sell their labour to capitalists and produce goods, but are paid less than the value of those goods because capitalists take part of that value when they take their profits. Analyses built on this foundation explain a great deal about capitalism's historical development, about the dynamic that drives it and the contradictions that have emerged, and why capitalism is probably in the last stages of self-destruction.

However, the issues that this book focuses on are rather different; chief among them are the unsatisfactory and inappropriate nature of development, the unacceptable relations between rich and poor nations, and the unjust nature of the global economy. These are mainly issues to do with the relations between nations, the distribution of wealth and resources, and the way in which the global economy determines these. The argument in Chapter 4 was that these matters are best explained in terms of market forces, and that little light can be thrown on them by analysing in terms of the mode of production. Part of the story is certainly the exploitation of Third World labour in plantations, mines and sweatshops, but one has to go well beyond this to explain why the surplus thus derived is not invested in appropriate development, why rich countries and their corporations are the main beneficiaries of the present world system, and why the global economy is unjust. These are essentially *distributive* effects, and are best explained in terms of market forces.

Market and exchange terms were explicitly rejected by Marx as bases for the analysis of capitalism. His point is valid and important: the essential nature of capitalism is indeed to do with the relations of production and the exploitation of labour, and he was right to warn against thinking that the essential nature of capitalism and what has driven its historical development can be grasped by concentrating on 'exchange', i.e., market phenomena. However, the foregoing argument has been that the *essence of development and inappropriate development is to be explained by concentrating on exchange, market forces, and distributive effects between nations and classes.*

Dependency and World Systems theorists do attempt to analyse in terms of exchange relations, but they have not gone on to give a clear and plausible explanation. The argument in Chapter 4 was that such an explanation can be given if one focuses on the way market forces produce inappropriate development and distribution, enrich the rich nations, and constitute the core of an unjust global economic system. The point being added here is that *these effects are only incidentally due to capitalism.* They occurred under other imperial systems before capitalism emerged, and even if all nations were suddenly to become socialist they would still participate in a global market system with the very same distributive effects that produce underdevelopment today. The USSR does not have a capitalist mode of production, but it participates in the global market system and thereby helps to produce deprivation and underdevelopment; when it buys grain on the world market it outbids hungry Third World people just as Western countries do.

Marxists have accused Dependency and World Systems Theories of operating in terms of relations between countries (e.g., talking about the way rich or 'core' countries exploit peripheral countries) when they see the essential fault in capitalism in terms of class relations, especially the relation between the working and the capitalist classes. But it is precisely relations between countries and how the global economy distributes wealth that must be the essential concern in an account of development.

All this can come as a shock to Marxists, who have tended to assume that they must have the key to the final explanation of underdevelopment. Marxist concepts certainly have a part in it, but not a leading role, because Marxist theory is not primarily about how wealth and productive capacity are distributed between nations, and how market forces and exchange relations determine inappropriate development.

Some writers have recognised that a full account of the state of development and what is wrong with it requires a combination of both analyses: the Marxist account of what happens at the micro-level, where surplus is derived from labour and the Dependency or World System approach to what happens to that surplus at the macro-level of development decisions, and distributive effects between and within nations.

MARX ON GROWTH AND APPROPRIATE DEVELOPMENT

Unfortunately there is another group of issues which lead to much less favourable conclusions about Marxist theory. Marx believed that a country must undergo a great deal of development before revolution became possible, and more importantly before the capacity for socialism could be established. He thought that socialism is not possible until there has been considerable 'development of the forces of production' – loosely speaking, technology.

What Marx means by 'development' in this context is essentially the same as the meaning assumed in conventional neo-classical theory. Development is equated with indiscriminate growth along a unidimensional path towards high material living standards. Contact with rich countries accelerates Third World countries along this path. This certainly results in exploitation, but their worst fate would be not to be exploited at all. No distinction is made between appropriate and inappropriate development, and there is no concept of any point at which sufficient growth has been achieved. The only choice is between fast and slow progress to the point of revolution, led by the merciless laws of history through the furnaces of mature capitalism.

Marx is in effect a modernisation theorist. There is no prospect other than the continuing destruction of non-western cultures. There is no room for, and indeed no value in, preserving the vast store of human culture at present precariously maintained by the remaining 'primitive' groups. Such cultures are impediments to the inevitable progression of capitalism. Universal proletarian culture is necessary; cultural diversity hinders revolution. As Marx said, 'The bourgeoisie, by the rapid improvement of all instruments of production, draws all, even the most barbaric nations into civilization,[173] and 'The country that is more developed industrially only shows to the less developed the image of its own future.'[174]

Admittedly there are certain aspects of traditional tribal or village life which most of us would want to see transcended. Yet it is precisely within the most 'primitive' cultures that we are beginning to recognise some of the most crucial attitudes and values for our survival, especially those relating to the treatment of nature, to co-operation ('retribalisation'), and to frugal material living standards.

Appropriate development theory holds out the hope that in order to reach a post-revolutionary and sustainable society it is not necessary to follow the long and dreadful path which Marx prescribed. The difference is largely to do with assumptions about the level to which living standards and the forces of production must develop before socialism becomes possible. The literature on appropriate development, the limits to growth and the conserver society make it clear that with respect to technology and living standards Marx was seriously mistaken. *Only very low levels of industrialisation, material affluence and technology are necessary before it becomes possible to organise highly satisfactory social systems and individual lifestyles.* The rich western countries probably passed those necessary levels at least a century ago. Some alternative lifestyle groups in the overdeveloped countries currently enjoy a very high quality of life (in their opinion) on per capita expenditures well below the poverty line.[175]

Conversely, the USA is nowhere near a transition to socialism – are we to believe that this is because its productive forces are not yet sufficiently developed? If so, the required level is far beyond any point that all the world's people can reach. Similarly, the occurrence of socialist revolutions and the rapid adoption of appropriate development strategies in countries with only very low levels of development of the productive forces, notably China, weakens the orthodox Marxist position. And how is it that the Amish, the Hutterites and the Israeli Kibbutzim have been able to establish such apparently highly effective socialist/communist societies based on the deliberate choice of relatively primitive lifestyles and technology?

Although Marx's account of communist society would seem to suggest modest material living standards in a zero growth economy, there is nothing in Marxist theory which enlists Marxists in 'limits to growth' demands this side of the revolution. This has rightly been a major point of attack from environmentalists.

There are many low and intermediate technologies whereby we could guarantee ourselves entirely sufficient material living standards with only a minute fraction of the industrialisation and sophisticated technology we employ today. Surely we must reject Marx's view that the forces of production have to reach sophisticated and highly productive levels before it becomes possible to achieve a satisfactory social order.

MARX ON THE TRANSITION

It is possible, however, that *in order to produce the necessary psychological conditions for transition* to post-capitalist society the forces of production must undergo much greater development. Marxist theory obscures the fact that revolutions are, 'in the last instance', due to *ideas, perceptions, and feelings*. This statement will strike orthodox Marxists as heresy, since their fundamental premise is that economic conditions rather than ideas or volition are the primary determinants of social change. Yet surely it makes more sense to say Marx showed that predictable changes in the economic substructure of capitalism are likely to produce experiences of deprivation and immiseration which in turn will produce the ideas, perceptions and feelings which finally lead people to take revolutionary action. Given that ideas and feelings must be the final links in the chain, we come to the question which has often been asked: is it not possible to develop those necessary ideas in a more direct, quick and painless way, via 'educational' activity. Many varieties of utopian socialists have argued in the affirmative. The orthodox Marxist view is that we must paradoxically grind our way to obscenely wasteful and potentially catastrophic higher levels of technical development before we will have generated the necessary psychological conditions for revolution, and therefore before it will become possible to come back down to the relatively low levels of technical development appropriate for a satisfactory social order. This is, for example, Kitching's view. '. . . human societies . . . must *pass through* a phase of industrialisation and urbanisation, of the large scale concentration of people (technology), and capital, in order to use the knowledge and productive power acquired in that process to create *afterwards* a smaller-scale, more democratic and less alienated world under communism.'[176] Kitching discusses the history of this debate, and notably its significance in pre-revolutionary Russia. Lenin, for instance, attacked the Narodniks for thinking that village socialism could be built directly and immediately, without having to go through capitalism.[177] Kitching follows Marx in insisting that there is no alternative to the long road[178]; he (Kitching) states the position effectively (but can hardly be said to offer a case in support of it).

As Kitching makes clear, the debate is also about the

need for industrialisation, and about whether 'socialism in one country' can be built, or whether nothing significant can be achieved until the whole world undergoes revolution. If the capacity of small regions to provide for themselves mostly using 'rural' technologies is as great as appropriate development theorists claim, then international support for socialist initiatives becomes much less crucial and the need for heavy and extensive industrialisation much less pressing.

Warren's writings have recently refuelled this classic issue. Marx believed that he had discovered the laws which history follows, including the sequence whereby capitalism would grind to maturity and collapse. Orthodox Marxists such as Warren confront us with the possibility that capitalism is such a massive system, harnessing such immense forces for the pursuit of accumulation, that there is no real choice other than to wait for it to self-destruct. They believe that it is pointless to work at persuading people to change to a different system, or indeed to start building alternatives here and now. They even believe that such efforts can only slow the necessary maturation process; hence Warren attacked anti-imperialist movements in the Third World because they were only likely to promote 'nationalist' capitalist development, and he attacked Dependency theory for supporting these movements.

There are very good reasons for hoping that Marx was wrong. To advance to the point where development of the forces of production have generated sufficient social damage to prompt the feelings that will trigger revolution is also to move further towards the irremediable destruction of the globe's resource base and ecosystems, and therefore to set more and more intractable social and technical problems for any post-revolutionary society. Each decade that passes sees the accumulation of ever greater problems of toxic waste, atmospheric pollution, nuclear waste, erosion, forest loss and genetic loss. In addition, the longer we experience affluence, consumerism and passivity, the more impoverished will be our capacity for individual and collective self-sufficiency and self-government, and our willingness to adopt the values and lifestyles essential for a sustainable, regionally self-sufficient conserver society.

The main grounds for believing that Marx was also wrong on the transition issue come again from the conserver society theorists. The 'revolution' they see as necessary is not one in which a vanguard can take power and lead us to salvation. *There is no chance whatsoever of establishing the conserver society or making it work until we have generated widespread public acceptance of conserver society perspectives and values.* People cannot be forced by any dictatorship of the proletariat to be genuinely committed to local ecosystems and communities, to co-operate and share conscientiously, to exercise civic responsibility, to identify with their town, and to forgo ecologically harmful luxuries. The simple, self-sufficient, co-operative alternative society this revolution is for can only come to be if most or all people first thoroughly understand why it is necessary – and willingly commit themselves to that alternative.

Many communal/conserver societies (monasteries, rural communes, kibbutzim) work very well at present primarily because their members are clear and committed regarding these key ideas and values. The viability of sustainable conserver societies is a *cultural* question, and therefore an educational question, not a technical or economic question. The current regression in 'socialist' countries (notably China) towards greater use of material incentives and market forces testifies to the general failure of these societies to progress far towards post-capitalist ideas and values. In particular, work motivation appears not to have advanced beyond the wage packet. Commitment to collectivist welfare and personal growth, let alone the welfare of local and global ecosystems, appear to have made little progress. Value changes of this sort are crucial prior conditions for the transition to a sustainable post-capitalist world order.

The concept of appropriate development also encourages us to side against the Marxist position on this issue. In a sense appropriate development strategies could very easily be pursued, since they draw upon locally available resources and require little in the way of scarce capital, energy imports or sophisticated technology. They could in many cases be instituted immediately: it is not necessary to wait for savings to accumulate, or for aid and external investment, or for trickle down. All that seems to stand in the way in most places is little more than a lack of awareness of the existence of appropriate options, or a failure to value alternative ways. Hence the technical simplicity of the alternative tempts one to conclude that if sufficient awareness and appreciation of conserver ways could be generated, transition could be achieved without having to go through 'maturation' and the death throes of capitalism.

The orthodox Marxist sequence assumes that the required awareness and values for a satisfactory society will be built during the long period of dictatorship of the proletariat *after* the revolution. The concept of appropriate development suggests that the order can be, indeed has to be, reversed. Appropriate development cannot take place unless ideas and values which contradict the capitalist world view first come to be held. If the analysis in previous chapters, especially Chapter 6, is sound, the transition to a sustainable society cannot possibly be undertaken unless there has first been a widespread repudiation of capitalist values, notably to do with affluent lifestyles, growth and accumulation. When capitalism collapses, the proletarian vanguard will surely take us off in the wrong direction again, chasing after affluent lifestyles and economic growth, unless we manage to get mistaken ideas out of everyone's head *before* the revolution. Hence the supreme importance of helping to spread appropriate ideas and values now. A wide variety of environmental, peace, appropriate technology, conserver, voluntary simplicity and new age movements are working hard at this task.

CHAPTER 9

The Alternative: Appropriate Development for Rich and Poor Countries

Since the early 1960s there has been a rapid growth of social movements concerned with the nature of the alternative: the sustainable or conserver society. These sources argue that there *are* viable and attractive alternative technologies, economic structures and lifestyles to which the developed countries and the Third World could move.

People are coming to see that what seemed like many separate problems – environment, peace, poverty, Third World underdevelopment, quality of life, resource depletion – are not only linked, but in fact are all largely caused by or are manifestations of the one basic problem: the growth and greed society. There is therefore one neat solution – change to a society which does not generate all these problems. You cannot put together plausible solutions to the problems now threatening us without facing up to the need for fundamental change in some of the basic values, lifestyles, systems and goals that have driven Western society for centuries, especially those to do with material living standards.

It is not surprising that many people cannot believe change of such magnitude is possible within the space of a few decades. What such people usually do not understand is that *there are alternatives*; there are abundant technologies, ideas and arrangements which could quite easily enable us to organise very satisfactory material lifestyles with a higher quality of life than most of us have now, yet with resource and environment costs that are a small fraction of present costs. The problem is not technical; we already have all the technologies we need. The main problem is that most people do not realise that many workable and attractive ways are available.

The same basic set of principles holds for thinking about alternative development in both rich and poor countries. Any vision of a just world order must be framed in terms of a general form of social organisation in which all people can share. We cannot tell the Third World to live simply while we do not. Nevertheless, it is convenient to sketch the implications for the rich world and the Third World separately.

APPROPRIATE DEVELOPMENT FOR THE RICH COUNTRIES

Any solution to the limits to growth problem has to involve an enormous reduction in per capita resource and energy use rates in the rich countries of the world. Consequently the first implication is to take advantage of the vast scope that exists for reduction in unnecessary production, through cutting down or eliminating many trivial products, designing goods to last and to be repaired, recycling, decentralising so that more people can get to work without cars, and reducing the resource cost of many of our systems, notably by moving food production closer to where food is consumed. The first principle must be the acceptance of far more simple and less affluent 'conserver' lifestyles.

Secondly, we could also greatly increase the self-sufficiency of households, local neighbourhoods, regions and nations, using alternative technologies (especially alternative energy sources, permacultures and earth building), planting 'edible urban landscapes' and urban forests, and enabling local committees to carry out many tasks presently performed by bureaucrats and professions. We could regenerate country towns, reduce the factory and office week, and increase time spent 'working' in a variety of backyards, local small businesses and community groups close to home. As we decentralise and phase out unnecessary production there will be far less need for the car, meaning that much derelict urban land and many little-used roads could be converted to gardens, ponds, meadows, woodlots and forest. We would therefore regenerate and enrich the suburbs as sources of production, community and leisure activity.

The central principle is the building of thriving, small-scale *regional economies* which are highly self-sufficient and integrated, with a minimum of importing and transporting into the region, and a maximum of independence and security from external economic fluctuations. It is absurd that in thousands of towns and cities within rich countries, millions of people go without jobs, goods and facilities, waiting for some corporation on another continent to order more steel or to open a subsidiary in their town, when those towns and cities have all the labour, talent, resources and capital to produce for themselves most if not all of the basic goods and services they need to ensure a satisfying way of life.

The third element is co-operation. Many goods and services can be provided by towns and neighbourhoods through sharing, pooling, co-operatives, rosters and community work periods (such as one day a month in voluntary work on an agreed project). This applies especially to 'welfare' services, including much of the care of old people and invalids. The organisation of these functions would involve people in the participatory government of their local areas.

The prerequisite for the conserver society is a shift from a value system focused on endlessly increasing affluence to one in which low but adequate material living standards are willingly accepted, without any desire for rises over time, and in which the core values are community, caring for the environment, creating, growing things and personal development.

Evidence on alternative lifestyles in developed countries indicates that huge reductions in per capita money and resource costs can be made by plausible lifestyle changes and access to at least a rudimentary regional economy. The reduction could fairly readily be to as one-fifth of present GNP per capital.[179] A reduction in resource use in the rich countries to one-third of present levels would mean a ninefold increase in the quantities available for the Third World.

There are many places where several of the required options have been practised for some time, such as Davis in California, the Kibbutzim of Israel, and in intentional rural communities. Yet there are very substantial non-technical problems blocking the necessary transition. The biggest of these is that it cannot be undertaken on a wide scale in a basically capitalist economy, since it involves not only shifting to an economy in which far less producing and consuming would take place than at present, but to a non-growth economy and a way of life concerned with goals other than constantly becoming richer in material or consumer terms. These principles are totally incompatible with a capitalist economy, which cannot function without the maximum possible amount of business activity and a constant increase over time in investment, production and consumption.

SATISFACTORY AND APPROPRIATE THIRD WORLD DEVELOPMENT

For the Third World, alternative or appropriate development means the reaffirmation of development based on village and regional self-sufficiency which many, notably Gandhi, have advocated for a long time, and which has been pursued in a wide variety of cases. 'Gandhi realised that the development model followed by the West was impossible . . .'

The argument in this book has been that two large recent bodies of literature, on the failure of growth and trickle down development and on the limits to growth, now combine to leave no doubt about the general form of the alternative model which has to become focal from here on. It is not surprising that during two or three decades of spectacular boom the 'indiscriminate growth and trickle down' model swept aside all the other options and was accepted without question. These two streams of literature now show that the conventional model is quite unacceptable and that it is necessary to concentrate on the highly self-sufficient village-based strategy. This is not to imply that a neat alternative strategy has been unambiguously established and requires no further evaluation; it is to identify the arena in which the search for satisfactory development goals and strategies must take place from here on.

'Attainment of a middle class lifestyle for the majority of the world's population is clearly an impossible goal.' p. 23. When defined in middle class terms, '. . . development is an impossibility. It simply cannot be achieved. Any effort for it can only aggravate the misery of absolute poverty.' p. 22.

S. Dasgupta, *Towards a Post R Development Era*, 1985.

The foregoing discussion and the considerable literature on appropriate technology suggest the following basic principles of appropriate Third World development.

1. **Focus on the concept of appropriateness**. Seek to develop only those things likely to raise the overall quality of life in view of local and global ecological, resource and justice considerations. Scrap the idea that development is a unidimensional matter of indiscrimi-

nate economic growth. Seek to *prevent* development and growth of inappropriate industries.

2. **Totally abandon Western affluence as a goal of development**. It is not possible and it is not desirable. Aim at the achievement of low but comfortable living standards for all on the lowest reasonable levels of non-renewable resource consumption.

3. **Attend more to social, political, environmental, cultural and human development than to merely economic development**. Beware of the dominant tendency to assume that economic development is all that needs attention.

4. **Start at the bottom**. Make existing development resources, especially capital and land, available to the people, so that they can identify their own priorities and plan their own strategies, employing those resources to meet their own needs. Harness their concern, labour and local knowledge.

5. **Maximise local economic self-sufficiency**. Encourage the development of integrated, small-scale regional economies, whereby a variety of small producers can provide most of the goods and services needed in the area, using locally available inputs. Seek to minimise transport and trade. Aim at maximum reasonable self-sufficiency and independence at all levels: village, regional, state and national. Minimise the need to export in order to import necessities, and maximise independence from the treacherous global economy.

6. **Small is beautiful**. Decentralise; democratise; devolve control to local regions and villages. Minimise dependence on foreign sources of capital, energy, spare parts and expertise. Maximise use of local inputs.

7. **Use appropriate technologies**. These will mostly be low, intermediate and alternative technologies processing locally available resources. Develop largely self-maintaining low-input systems, such as permaculture. Use labour-intensive ways. Avoid as far as poss-

end to the privileges currently enjoyed by these groups, so it is not surprising that such strenuous efforts are made by them to prevent the success of any alternative to the conventional growth and trickle down approach.

A THIRD WAY

It should by now be clear why the alternative is best described as a 'third way', which rejects the capitalist or free enterprise way and the typical socialist/communist way with its reliance on a massive authoritarian state apparatus running a centralised, industrialised and growth-obsessed socio-economic system. The third way adopts some of the best elements from each of these two systems. It can incorporate a considerable amount of free enterprise in the form of small private and cooperative 'firms' operating to some extent according to market forces within carefully set and monitored guidelines. On the other hand it must involve rational social discussion and planning of the basic economic structures and priorities in view of the welfare of human beings and ecosystems. If there is one thing that the examination of the present state of the world makes clear, it is that these decisions cannot be left to free enterprise, the profit motive and the market. Some form of 'socialist' planning of the *basic* priorities (and nationalisation or at least close control of the few large firms to be retained) must be accepted.

But in most respects the third way is very different from capitalism or socialism as we know them. The third way is essentially to do with the establishment of secure, independent, highly self-sufficient, small scale, *regional economies* based mostly on local inputs of labour and other resources, and on low but adequate material living standards within a zero growth economy.

At this point a Marxist might reply, 'But how can we contemplate retaining a significant role for the market and production for profit, the very factors so clearly responsible for most of the trouble we are in?' This raises the very difficult question of the huge *cultural* transition from the self-interest and greed which now predominate to the non-material and far more 'collectivist' or altruistic values that must eventually be generally held if we are to attain a satisfactory social order. The distance between the two is currently so great that we cannot expect to traverse it in one step or in a short time. The third way represents ; first step in the right direction, but one which accepts th impossibility of a complete and sudden abandonment the values involving self-interest, profit, greed and accur lation that have driven our society for five hundred yea Hence it accepts a place for free enterprise mainly of th small business variety, where the concern is not solely or primarily capital accumulation, but being in control of one's own venture and providing a worthwhile service.

The eventual goal should, I believe, be something like the concept of communism which Marx put forward, where we all 'work' or contribute as best we can in view of our varied abilities but where we are all 'paid' according to our needs. Thus if you are stronger than I am you will do more in a day's work, but if I feel the cold more than you I can have two jumpers where you might only need one. Material rewards would be totally irrelevant. Our regional economies would very easily produce all we need for very satisfactory material living standards on something like one or two day's work a week, and we would then just take all the goods we needed, 'free', from community stores. Greed would be meaningless; what would be the point of taking three jumpers if you only needed one? Such a conception of 'communism' (clearly unrelated to present Soviet or Eastern European practice) only endorses the principles whereby a good family, or a convent, or a kibbutz functions at present. Economics too would then be almost irrelevant, and most of our time and energy would be devoted to far more important things, such as community development, creativity, caring for the environment, and learning and growing as a person.

The third way should be seen as a possible first step on the long journey from our present acquisitive and selfish culture to a convivial, humane and caring culture. This problem of determining the most promising strategy for transition is very important but very difficult. The foregoing argument has attempted to hold open the possibility of a rather non-Marxist transition which (a) attends to the cultural problem (value change) now rather than after the 'revolution'; (b) does not necessarily depend on a violent revolution; and (c) assumes the possibility of a gradual phasing out of production for profit, the market, greed and accumulation in which the first step (to the third way) retains aspects of the free enterprise spirit. However it is quite possible that hard line Marxists, who would see the third way as inexcusably naïve, are right in believing that the break will inevitably be abrupt and violent and must involve ruthless leadership.

THE MISSING LINK: THE SUFFICIENCY OF ALTERNATIVE TECHNOLOGIES

Most development theorists have so far rejected any suggestion of striving to minimise involvement in national and international economic networks, or of aiming for a high degree of national and local self-sufficiency. 'Autarchy' is usually dismissed as a naïve mistake. Certainly it is *if* one continues to hold conventional development goals such as the eventual achievement of heavy industrialisation, high levels of GNP and western affluent lifestyles. But conservers begin with a totally different view of the goals of development focusing on frugality, sufficiency and stability.

Conservers understand two crucial points which contradict the basic assumptions of conventional economists. Firstly, given sensible reorganisation, co-operative systems, restored ecosystems and conserver values, only *remarkably low levels of consumption of resources are necessary* for the achievement of quite satisfactory material living standards and a high quality of life. Secondly, *existing alternative and appropriate technologies provide in abundance the necessary resources.*

It is difficult to give sufficient emphasis to these points. Most people in our affluent society, and especially most economists, have little idea of how easily we could derive a way of life that is materially modest yet entirely sufficient, while being socially and spiritually rich in terms of creativity, community and personal growth. The most fully worked out ideas are probably those to be found within the permaculture approach to the design of human living spaces.[182] This involves the development of complex, integrated, permanent ecosystems based on tree crops rather than annuals, which require low or zero inputs of nonrenewable resources, and which ensure that much of the 'work' required to maintain the system is carried out by the natural processes within the system. For example water can be stored and regulated by the forests and pests can be controlled by animals and companion planting. Central to the approach is the use of extensive ranges of plants and animals providing an abundant variety of foods, chemicals, medicines, fibres, fuel, timber and other materials. Carob and honey locust trees can produce ten times the Australian average wheat yield per hectare. They do not need replanting every year, and they thrive in dry stony regions.

Integrated systems can take advantage of many overlaps and niches. Animal and human wastes can be recycled through methane gas producing units to enrich ponds producing a range of fish, fowl and plants. Small animals can be fed by food falling from varieties of trees planted to fruit in sequence, while at the same time consuming pests, cultivating, weeding and fertilising, and themselves producing food. Acquaculture can achieve thirty times the food production per hectare typical of land-based systems. Ponds can purify town sewage output while converting the nutrients to useful purposes; salvinia, a pond 'weed', can produce sixty times the biomass of a wheat crop, and can be harvested for alcohol or methane production as well as for compost.

Housing is one of the most effective areas for illustrating alternatives that are far cheaper than conventional ways.

Earth building can reduce building costs to 10% of those associated with conventional housing, and even lower costs in non-renewable resources. Taking average 1987 construction costs for a new house in Sydney, and typical financing arrangements, the conventional home owner will pay out around $250,000 over 25 years (including payments of interest and taxes on earnings). He or she will work something like 9½ years *just to pay the interest to the capitalists whose money was borrowed!* Yet there are many perfectly satisfactory houses built by alternative lifestylers in Australia – from mud brick for example – for less than $7000. The Victorian Ministry of Housing has a scheme whereby home builders are assisted with the construction of their own mud brick houses. One of their designs is for a $14,000 house.

Water storage via small tanks, and especially via the water holding capacity of well wooded hills, involves capital costs which are a fraction of those of conventional big dams. The annual water *delivery* cost (excluding the cost of building dams, mains and pumping stations) per house for Sydney in 1987, $280, is around one-third of the entire cost of a permanent household water storage and supply plant involving roof collection of rainwater, a concrete tank and a small wind operated pump.

Sewage treatment provides another glaring example of the scope for savings. Sewage treatment systems are extraordinarily expensive, yet there is *no need at all* for domestic sewer systems. All household wastes can be recycled to local gardens through simple 'garbage gas' digesters which produce methane to run fridges, lights and small engines.

The scope for making cities highly self-sufficient in food is far greater than is commonly assumed. 'At least six Chinese cities produce within their boundaries more than 85% of their vegetable supplies in part by recycling nutrients from human wastes and garbage.'[183] The 'edible landscape' concept involves the dense planting of urban areas with productive plants, home gardens, community gardens, and commercial market gardens and orchards. In Village Homes California, commercial gardens have been planned within a housing subdivision, and much free fruit is obtained from roadside trees. Simply relocating market gardens on city wasteland would reduce the cost of food by as much as 70%, while enabling the recycling of food wastes to the soil.

These dense, integrated, permanent, largely self-maintaining ecosystems can provide the inputs for a wide range of small and intermediate technology 'firms' producing for local consumption. They are therefore the base on which highly self-sufficient regional economies can be built, since by nature they reduce the need for imported materials, energy and goods. There is no argument against sophisticated or high tech research and systems *per se*, so long as these are appropriate in terms of resources and environmental needs.

The conserver's most difficult task is to convey how easily most of the things needed for modest but satisfactory material living standards can be derived from existing alternative technologies, not to mention what could be achieved by further research in these relatively neglected fields. It is especially urgent that the potential abundance of local systems and alternative technologies should become much more widely appreciated within development circles. Such strategies can provide Third World villages in even the most impoverished and difficult regions with most if not all of the sources of food and materials required for at least reasonable material living standards, and within a relatively short period.

Most development theorists, radical as well as conventional, seem to have little or no idea of the potential for appropriate development inherent in these existing alternative technologies. Most recommend the acceptance of decades of further suffering on the part of billions of people until trickle down saves them or until capitalism self-destructs, essentially because they do not understand that we already have the ideas and techniques necessary to enable those people to build satisfactory economies for themselves within a few years, and in many cases within a few months.

Several of the alternative technologies mentioned in this section are already in operation at my own relatively self-sufficient 'homestead', which is being developed as an alternative lifestyle demonstration site. A two-bedroom cottage, built to local council standards, cost around $7,500 (1988 $). Per capita living costs are under one-quarter of the national average – well below the poverty line. Most of the buildings and machinery were constructed using simple tools and recycled material. All nutrients are recycled to gardens and animal pens. The experience gained in this venture over some twenty years leaves me in no doubt as to how easily and cheaply people in the Third World and in the rich world could ensure for themselves quite satisfactory and secure lifestyles.

THE TRANSITION IS UNDER WAY

In the last twenty years many social movements have emerged under the general heading of a transition to a sustainable society. The most impressive recent examples have been the rise of the Green parties in a number of countries. Many groups previously working for apparently separate campaigns – the environment, or peace, or poverty – are coming to see that their concerns are linked, and that there is only one long term solution – a transition to a conserver society.

Although we have a very long way to go, we have come a long way in a mere twenty years. There is now considerable recognition that our society has enormous problems which are basically due to faulty values and structures, and that only fundamental change can solve these problems. Survey evidence often reveals remarkably high levels of insight into these issues. In the 1970s various surveys found that a majority of Americans recognised the need for the rich countries to live more simply.[187]

By far the most important contribution anyone can make

to the transition is to commit oneself to the long-term task of spreading awareness of the crucial themes, especially the fact that ours is not a sustainable or morally acceptable society, that de-development is necessary, that Third World development has to abandon the conventional path and focus on appropriateness, and that there are alternatives to which the rich countries could move.

The problem is an educational one. We cannot hope to achieve a transition to a sustainable world order unless and until most people come to understand why fundamental change is essential, and come to see that the alternative ways not only make survival sense, but represent an attractive way to live. There is nothing more important for socially concerned individuals to do than to work at this task, perhaps for decades to come.

This does not mean that we should cease our efforts on specific 'bandaid' projects, such as protecting the last of the rainforest from the bulldozers, but unless we make the transition our supreme goal, and eventually achieve it, then all the effort that goes into saving this or that bit of forest will have been insignificant. Fortunately our specific bandaiding campaigns give us ideal platforms from which to raise awareness about the need for transition. While protesting in front of the bulldozers we can make sure that we also explain that the eventual solution to problems like forest destruction has to be a change to a society that does not require endless increases in the consumption of woodchips.

People working in the development field are in an excellent position to help us with this educational task because the last thirty years have provided overwhelming evidence against two of the most basic premises of the growth and greed society: (a) that making the pursuit of economic growth the supreme social goal will raise the real living standards of all and solve social problems, and (b) that it is possible for all to rise to the living standards of the developed countries. Focusing attention on the absurdity of these assumptions as foundations for Third World development, and on the need to think about what might constitute appropriate development there, is a very effective way to jog people in the rich world into asking the same questions about their own society.

It is important to distinguish this educational task from the business of actually establishing aspects of the required alternative society here and now, or working for appropriate development in the Third World. It is excellent that effort is at present going into setting up these sorts of arrangements, but this is at present not the most important thing to do. In fact it is quite possible for these sorts of ventures to make little or no contribution to the revolution. It is relatively unimportant just to get one more co-op or community garden going; we are not going to transform this society simply by steadily adding to the number of alternative structures in existence. This will sooner or later grind to a halt against the vast bulk of supermarket consumers who couldn't care less about community gardens, and see them as the hobby interest of rather weird fringe groups. There is no chance that we will eventually have community gardens everywhere *unless the majority of people come to understand why this is necessary*, and therefore give political support for the radical urban rezoning and the digging up of many roads that has to take place before cities can become edible landscapes. Certainly one of the most effective educational strategies involves setting up alternative experiments and using them as educational devices.[185] But we must be clear that *what matters is their educational use, not simply having one more alternative on the ground*.

The crucial task therefore is to help as many people as possible to understand the issues; it is not just trying to get more alternative projects going in the rich countries or more appropriate development going in the Third World. The two tasks need not conflict, but there is a danger that they will. There is a strong tendency for all the available energy to go into establishing yet another alternative or appropriate scheme while none of it goes into raising public awareness.

This is often seen as a disappointing answer to the question 'What is the best strategy?' It is understandable that more spectacular and quicker strategies are wished for, but there is really no other way. The problem is inescapably one of awareness. We will get nowhere until most people have come to understand the unsustainable nature of our society, the need for fundamental change, and the existence of alternatives. Nothing is more important than to contribute to increasing that awareness, and to commit ourselves to that dull and thankless task in whatever arenas we have access to, for decades to come.

After three hundred years of virile growth, and a long boom in which doubt was inconceivable, the growth and greed society has suddenly burst into an era of problems, chaos and uncertainty, giving us an unprecedented opportunity to move to more sensible arrangements. Whether or not we manage to take that opportunity will depend upon whether enough of us devote ourselves to the crucial educational task. Unless many more of us do adopt this as our chief long-term priority, there is little chance of us making it to a just, peaceful and ecologically sustainable world order.

APPENDIX

A Summary of Key Themes for Development Educators and Development Agencies

Unfortunately much of the effort of development educators and non-government aid organisations does not go into raising, let alone stressing, the themes argued in this book. Indeed their activities often implicitly assume that some variety of the conventional development strategy is acceptable. What follows is a summary list of the major themes argued in the book, which it is hoped will facilitate the work of development educators and agencies in framing appropriate programs.

1. **The development issue must be seen as part of the much wider issue of our unsustainable society.**

2. **The commitment to affluence and growth and to the market system in the overdeveloped countries are the major factors generating the big global problems facing us:** environment, resource and energy scarcity, nuclear energy, hunger, poverty, injustice, conflict and quality of life.

3. **The global economic system is massively unjust:** it delivers most of the world's wealth to the rich few.

4. **The Third World problem is essentially one of distribution:** most people do not have access to a fair

share of the world's resources. Market forces are the main cause; they inevitably result in appallingly bad distributions.

5. **The affluent living standards of people in rich countries are therefore directly connected to the poverty of most people in the world:** we could not be so affluent if we were not taking most of the resources and gearing much of the Third World's productive capacity to our purposes.

6. **Satisfactory development is not occurring and it is not likely to result from the conventional approach:** highly inappropriate development is taking place, development in the interests of the rich.

7. **Trickle down effects are miniscule:** is would take centuries of continued boom conditions to raise Third World people to our present living standards, even if resource and environment conditions held up.

8. **The conventional 'indiscriminate growth and trickle down someday' approach to development is bankrupt.**

9. **It is not possible for all the world's people to have the high living standards that people in the rich countries have now.**

10. **Satisfactory development for the Third World is not possible unless the rich countries move to more simple lifestyles,** to the zero-growth conserver economy that would enable them to live on something like their fair share of the world's resources.

11. **The rich must live more simply so that the poor may simply live.**

12. **The conventional development approach brings forth brutal repression in many parts of the Third World**: our affluence is connected with this repression.

13. **Long term global peace is not possible unless**

global justice is achieved: and that is not possible unless the rich countries move over.

14. **There are alternative ways to which we could easily shift, if most people wanted to do so:** these ways would enable a sustainable, just and peaceful world order, yielding a higher quality of life than most people experience now.

REFERENCES IN THE TEXT

Chapter 2: Conditions in the Third World (pp.8–37)

1. McGowan and Kordan, 1981
2. Kloby, 1987, p.6
3. Todaro, 1985, pp.29–30
4. Berryman, 1985
5. George, 1976, p.35; Freedom from Hunger Campaign, 1983; *New Internationalist*, Aug. 1982, p.9
6. Eckholm, 1976; *Ceres*, March/April 1977; UNICEF, 1977, p.4
7. Lipton, 1977
8. Todaro, 1981, p.204
9. Reutlinger, 1977
10. Brown, 1987, p.134
11. Brown, 1987, p.135
12. Brown, 1987, p.36
13. McGutcheon, 1979, p.39; Trainer, 1985, p.117; Lean, 1978
14. Todaro, 1985, p.288
15. Todaro, 1985, p.290
16. Murdoch, 1980, p.95
17. Todaro, 1985, p.293; Murdoch, 1980, p.187
18. Barney, 1980, p.2
19. World Bank, 1986, pp.190–191
20. Murdoch, 1980, p.117
21. Trainer, 1985, pp.209–210
22. Brown, 1987, p.13
23. Brown, 1987, p.126

24. Brown, 1987, p.124
25. World Bank, 1986, p.78
26. Brown, 1987, p.140
27. Brown, 1985, p.40
28. Murdoch, 1980, p.82; see also pp.37, 58, 63
29. Brown, 1987, pp.3, 22
30. Dammann, 1979, p.168
31. *UNCTAD Dossier*, April 1987, p.2

Chapter 3: Is Development Occurring? (pp.38–56)

32. World Bank, 1986, pp.15, 181
33. UNICEF, 1987, p.122
34. World Bank, 1986, p.226
35. Seligson, 1984, p.401
36. Morello, 1983
37. Morawetz, 1977
38. Harle, 1979; Sell and Kuntz, 1986; Todaro, 1985; *South*, April 1986, p.1
39. *South*, Jan. 1987, p.39; for similar figures see UNICEF, 1987, p.108
40. *UN Statistical Yearbook*, 1983/4, p.9
41. Brown, 1987, p.29
42. Langmore, 1987, p.24
43. UNICEF, 1987
44. World Bank, 1980 and 1986
45. Kuznets, 1968
46. Loehr and Powelson, 1981, p.129; Chenery, 1982, p.329
47. Arndt, 1983
48. Trainer, 1986a
49. Trainer, 1985, p.81
50. Brown, 1987, p.10
51. Brown, 1987, p.13
52. Ehrlich, 1977, pp.27–32; FAO, 1981, p.45
53. Browett, 1986; Park, 1981, p.115; Hettne, 1983; Cline, 1982
54. Warren, 1973; 1980

55. Pilkington, 1981, p.501
56. Beinfeld and Godfrey, 1982; see also Petras, 1986
57. Fitt *et al.*, 1978, p.161; Smith, 1980, p.90
58. Browett, 1985, p.795; Wheelwright, 1980, p.52 agrees
59. Browett, 1986, p.406; Browett, 1985, p.795
60. Worsley, 1980, p.327
61. Bauer, 1979, is the notable champion

Chapter 4: Underdevelopment (pp.57–80)

62. Toh, 1986; Bergin, 1986; Farrelly, 1987
63. Murdoch, 1980, p.98 estimates 37 million tonnes
64. Dammann, 1979, p.95
65. See for example Smith, 1980, p.14; Smith, 1982, p.13;
    Amin, 1976, p.189; Burbach and Flynn, 1980, p.11.
66. Abercrombie, 1982

Chapter 5: Exploring Inappropriate Development
(pp.81–116)

67. Trainer, 1985, pp.145–146
68. Bornschier and Chase-Dunn, 1985; in addition to
    their own evidence these authors note that fourteen
    of the fifteen studies they review come to the same
    conclusions; see also Lall and Streeten, 1977;
    Rothgeb, 1984; Bornschier, 1980; Bornschier *et al.*,
    1978; Chase-Dunn, 1975
69. Trainer, 1985, p.149
70. Bornschier and Chase-Dunn, 1985, p.134
71. Herman, 1982, p.107
72. Bornschier and Chase-Dunn, 1985, p.11
73. Vaitsos, 1974
74. *New Internationalist*, Dec. 1976, p.15; Muller, 1979,
    pp.258–259; Haslemere Group, *Who Needs the Drug
    Companies?*, p.10
75. Harrison, 1979
76. Burnett, 1979, p.13
77. Todaro, 1985, p.370
78. Morello, 1983; International Union of Food and
    Allied Workers Associations, 1984

79. *Malaya*, 11 March 1985, p.76
80. 'Weighing the Pros and Cons of Asian processing zones', *Development and Cooperation*, 3, May–June 1984, pp.31–33
81. *New Internationalist*, Nov. 1979, p.76
82. Harrington, 1977, p.236
83. Griffin and Gurley, 1985, document no fall between 1945 and 1975, but a fall thereafter (p.114); see also Osterfeld, 1982
84. Higgott, 1981
85. Bornschier and Chase-Dunn, 1985, p.140
86. Waddell, 1979
87. Chomsky and Herman, 1979, p.44
88. Todaro, 1985, p.353
89. *Australian Development Studies Newsletter*, Dec. 1987, p.25
90. Murdoch, 1980, p.260
91. George, 1988, p.34
92. Payer, 1976, p.65
93. Quoted in *Development Dialogue* 2, 1980
94. George, undated, p.18.
95. Kent, 1985
96. Murdoch, 1980, p.237; George, 1976, p.39; Trainer, 1985, p.141
97. Murdoch, 1980, pp.297–298
98. Borgstrom, 1969, p.311

Chapter 6: The Limits to Growth Perspective (pp.117–136)

99. Trainer, 1985, offers a summary of the argument as it stood in the early 1980s
100. Galtung, 1981, quotes an estimate of 214 million Cokes consumed daily
101. *Rodale Press Newsletter*, 1981, p.1
102. *Australian Society*, June 1987, p.30
103. For details of the derivation of this conclusion see Trainer, 1985, Chapters 3 and 4
104. Trainer, 1985, Chapter 4; Trainer 1984

105. Guppy, 1984
106. Myers, 1987
107. Skinner, 1985
108. Trainer, 1985, Chapter 10
109. Chapman and Roberts, 1983; Trainer, 1986a
110. For a discussion of the 'technical fix' view, see Trainer, 1985, Chapter 10
111. Sharp and Trainer, 1984; Trainer, 1985, Chapter 8; Trainer, 1987
112. Easterlin, 1972; see also Trainer, 1985, Chapter 9
113. Hirsch, 1977, p.11
114. Polanyi, 1985; see also the discussions of Polanyi in Dalton (ed.), 1971; Heilbronner, 1976, p.122; Hunt and Sherman, 1972, pp.8, 12, 13

Chapter 7: Maintaining Your Empire (pp.137–176)

115. Magdoff, 1969, pp.47–48; Geldicks, 1977; Eckes, 1979, p.241; Cameron, 1973, pp.10–12
116. Mesarovic, 1975, p.84
117. Anderson, 1976, p.154
118. Slee, 1976
119. Govett and Govett, 1977, p.9
120. UN Conference on Trade and Development, 1976, p.13
121. ABC News, 8 July, 1987
122. Quoted in Chomsky, 1986, p.48.
123. Chomsky, 1986, p.50
124. Jenkins, 1970
125. Arrighi, 1982, p.95
126. Galtung, 1981; Sivard, quoted in Chomsky, 1986, p.216
127. Klare, 1977
128. *ibid*, p.224
129. Herman, 1982
130. Chomsky and Herman, 1979
131. Chomsky, 1986
132. Chomsky, 1979, p.262; see also Herman, 1982, p.16

133. *The Guardian*, 17 April 1977; Herman, 1982, p.127
134. Herman, 1982, p.115
135. W. Moyer, 'De-developing the United States', *Alternatives*, 1973
136. Chomsky, 1986, p.287
137. Blasier, 1983, pp.78, 92
138. Blasier, 1983, p.44
139. Berryman, 1985, p.67
140. Chomsky, 1986, p.57
141. Chomsky, 1986, pp.52, 54, 57, 71
142. Blasier, 1983, p.183
143. Blasier, 1983, p.8
144. See for example Chomsky, 1986, pp.207ff.
145. Garrison and Shivpuri, 1983; Wolfe, 1984; Halliday, 1982; Kaplan, 1977; Prins, 1983; Lens, 1979; Chomsky, 1982; Mack, 1982
146. Quoted in Chomsky, 1986, p.86
147. Berryman, 1985, p.21
148. Blasier, 1983, pp.78, 92, 95, 102
149. Blasier, 1983, p.99
150. Blasier, 1983, p.78
151. Blasier, 1983, p.95
152. Blasier, 1983, pp.132, 145
153. Berryman, 1985, p.21; Blasier, 1983, p.93
154. Blasier, 1983, pp.153, 154
155. Blasier, 1983, p.153
156. Herman, 1982, p.33
157. This is Cesar's situation, portrayed in the BBC documentary 'Bolivia: The Tin Mountain'; see also Galeano, 1973, pp.166–167; Nash, 1979
158. Wallerstein, 1979; Thompson, 1983
159. Ashley, 1980; Choucri and North, 1975; Nelson and Olin, 1979; Organski and Kugler, 1980; Liska, 1968
160. Kloby, 1987; Piggott, 1984; Haskell, 1978

Chapter 8: Clarifying Radical Development Theory
(pp.177–194)

161. Toh, 1986; Farrelly, 1987; Bergin, 1986
162. Howe, 1983, p.23
163. Browett, 1987 argues that the situation is due to a mistaken quest for 'grand theory', or relatively wide and comprehensive frameworks. However, the argument in this book is for such a framework
164. Browett, 1985
165. World Bank, 1986, p.16
166. Notably Warren, 1973; 1980, who insists that the Third World is achieving normal, and indeed fairly rapid, capitalist development
167. Amin, 1976, refers to the notion of distorted development
168. Harrison, 1979
169. Warren, 1973; 1980
170. Baran, 1957; Baran and Sweezy, 1966; Frank, 1967
171. Brenner, 1977
172. Trainer, 1985
173. Marx, 1968, p.39
174. Marx, 1905, p.13
175. Trainer, 1984; Trainer, 1985, Chapter 12
176. Kitching, 1982, p.180
177. See also Macfarlane, 1985, p.32.
178. Kitching, 1982, p.180

Chapter 9: The Alternative (pp.195–211)

179. Trainer, 1984; Trainer, 1985, Chapter 5
180. *The Ecologist* 15, 5/6, 1985, p.211; there is extensive evidence in support of this point, see for example McRobie, 1981
181. Mollison and Holmgren, 1978, p.8
182. Mollison, 1979; Mollison and Holmgren, 1978
183. Brown, 1987, p.48
184. Trainer, 1985, pp.280–281
185. F.E. Trainer, 'What We Need Most Of All Right Now', *Green Teacher* 2, 1986

Bibliography

Abercrombie, K. (1982), 'Intensive livestock feeding', *Ceres*, Jan.–Feb. pp.38–42.

Amin, S. (1976), *Unequal Development*, London, Harvester Press.

Anderson, C. (1976), *The Sociology of Survival: Social Problems of Growth*, Homewood, Ill., Dorsey Press.

Arndt, H.W. (1983), 'The trickle-down myth', *Economic Development and Cultural Change*, Oct. 32, 1, pp.1–10.

Arrighi, G. (1982), 'A crisis of hegemony', in S. Amin (ed), *Dynamics of Global Crisis*, New York, Monthly Review Press.

Baily, S. (1976), *The US and the Development of South America*.

Baran, P. (1957), *The Political Economy of Growth*, Harmondsworth, Penguin.

Baran, P. and P. Sweezy (1966), *Monopoly Capital*, New York, Monthly Review Press.

Barnett, D.W. (1979), *Minerals and Energy in Australia*, Sydney, Cassell.

Bauer, P.T. (1971), *Dissent on Development*, London, Weidenfeld and Nicolson.

Bellow, W. (1982), *Development Debacle*. Washington, Inst. for Food and Dev. Policy.

Bergin, P.I. (1986), *Development Education in NSW State High Schools: An Evaluative Study*, M.Ed. Thesis, University of New England.

Berryman, P. (1985), *Inside Central America*, New York, Pantheon.

Bienfeld, M. and M. Godfrey (eds) (1982), *The Struggle for Development*, New York, Wiley.

Blasier, C. (1983), *The Giants Rival*, Pittsburgh, University of Pittsburgh Press.

Borgstrom, G. (1969), *Too Many*, New York, Macmillan.

Bornschier, V. (1980), 'Multinational corporations and economic growth', *Journal of Development Economics* 7, pp.191–210.

Bornschier, V. *et al.* (1978), 'Cross national evidence of the effects of foreign investment and aid on economic growth and inequality: A survey of findings and reanalysis', *American Journal of Sociology* 84, 3, Nov., pp.651–683.

Bornschier, V. and C. Chase-Dunn (1985), *Transnational Corporations and Under Development*, New York, Praeger.

Brandt, W. (1980), *North South*, London, Pan.

Browett, J. (1985), 'The Newly Industrialising Countries and radical theories of development', *World Development* 13, 7, pp.789–803.

Browett, J. (1986), 'Industrialisation in the global periphery: The significance of the new industrialising countries of East and South East Asia', *Environment and Planning* 4, pp.401–418.

Browett, J. (1987), 'Crises for global capitalism and crisis in development thinking', Duplicated MS, Politics, Flinders University.

Brown, L.R. (1985), *The State of the World*, New York, Norton.

Burbach, R. and P. Flynn (1980), *Agribusiness in the Americas*, New York, Monthly Review Press.

Caldwell, M. (1977), *The Wealth of Some Nations* London, Zed.

Cameron, E. (1973), 'The contribution of the United States to national and world mineral supplies', in E. Cameron (ed), *The Mineral Position of the United States, 1975–2000*, Wisconsin, University of Wisconsin Press.

Cassen, R. *et al.* (1985), *Does Aid Work?*, Oxford, Clarendon.

Chapman, P. and F. Roberts (1983), *Metal Resources and Energy*, London, Butterworth.

Chase-Dunn, C. (1975), 'The effects of international economic dependence on development and inequality: A cross-national study.' *American Sociological Review* 40, Dec., pp.720–738.

Chenery, H. (1982), 'Poverty and Progress', in G.A. Almond *et al.* (eds), *Progress and Its Discontents*, Berkeley, University of California Press, Chapter 15.

Chomsky, N. (1979), *The Political Economy of Human Rights, Vol. 1: The Washington Connection and Third World Fascism*, Boston, South End.

Chomsky, N. (1981), 'The Cold War and the Superpowers', *Monthly Review*, Nov., pp.1–10.

Chomsky, N. (1982), *Towards a New Cold War*, London, Sinclair Brown.

Chomsky, N. (1986), *Turning the Tide; U.S. Intervention in Central America*, London, Pluto.

Cline, W. (1982), 'Can the East Asian Model of Development be Generalised', *World Development* 10, 2.

Cockroft, J. *et al.* (1973), *Dependence and Underdevelopment.*

Dalton, G. (ed.), *Primitive, Archaic and Modern Economics*, Boston, Beacon.

Dammann, E. (1979), *Future in Our Hands*, London, Pergamon.

Dasgupta, S. (1985), *Towards a Post Development Era*, London, Mittal.

Dennis, R. and R. Landsness (1978), *The Economics of Hunger.*

Diwan, R.K. and D. Livingston (1979), *Alternative Development Strategies and Appropriate Technology*, New York, Pergamon.

Easterlin, R.A. (1972), 'Does economic growth improve the human lot? Some empirical evidence', in P.A. David and M.W. Reder (eds), *Nations and Households in Economic Growth*, Stanford, Stanford University Press.

Eckes, A.E. (1979), *The United States and the Global Struggle for Minerals*, Austin, Texas, University of Texas Press.

Eckholm, E. (1976), *The Two Faces of Malnutrition*, World-watch Paper 9, Worldwatch Institute.

Eckholm, E. (1979), *The Dispossessed of the Earth*, World-watch Paper 30.

Ehrlich, P., A. Ehrlich, and T. Holdren (1977), *Ecoscience*, San Francisco, Freeman.

Farrelly, T. (1987), *Technocrats for Rural Development? A Study of Third World Students in Selected Australian Universities*, M.Ed. Thesis, University of New England.

Fitt, Y., *et al.* (1978), *The World Economic Crisis*, London, Zed Books.

Food and Agriculture Organisation (1981), *The State of Food and Agriculture*, 1980, Rome, United Nations.

Frank, A.G. (1967), *Capitalist Development in Latin America*, New York, Monthly Review Press.

Freedom from Hunger Campaign (1982), *Development Handbook*.

Freedom from Hunger Campaign (1983), *Action*, Jan–March, (F.F.H.C. Newsletter).

French-Davis, R. (1987), 'Latin American debit:debtor-creditor relations', *Third World Quarterly*, Oct., pp.1167–1175.

Fuller, R. (1980), *Inflation*, Worldwatch Paper 34.

Galeano, E. (1973), *The Open Veins of Latin America*, New York, Monthly Review Press.

Galtung, J. (1981), 'Global processes and the world in the 1980's', Chapter 5 in W.L. Hollist and J.N. Rosenau (eds), *World Systems Structure*, Beverly Hills, Sage.

Geldicks, A. (1977), 'Raw materials: The Achilles heel of American imperialism?', *Insurgent Sociologist* VII, 4, Fall, pp.3–14.

George, S. (undated), *Corporate Control of Food in the Third World*, Sydney, Australian Freedom From Hunger Campaign.

George, S. (1977), *How the Other Half Dies*, Harmondsworth, Penguin.

George, S. (1988), 'Oh! What a Lovely Debt!', *Australian*

Society, April, pp.34–35.

Griffin, K., and J. Gurley (1985), 'Radical analyses of imperialism, the Third world, and the transition to socialism: A survey article', *Journal of Economic Literature* XXIII, Sept, pp.1089–1143.

Guppy, N. (1984), 'Tropical deforestation: A global view', *Foreign Affairs* 4, Spring, pp.928–966.

Halliday, F. (1982), *Threat From the East?*, Harmondsworth, Penguin.

Haq, M. Ul (1976), *The Poverty Curtain*, Baltimore, Johns Hopkins Press.

Harrington, M. (1977), *The Vast Majority*, London, Macmillan.

Harrison, P. (1979), *Inside the Third World*, Harmondsworth, Pelican.

Harle, V. (1978), *The Political Economy of Food*, Westmead, Saxon House.

Hartman, B. and J. Boyce (1979), *Needless Hunger*, San Francisco, I.D.F.P.

Heilbronner, R. (1976), *Business Civilization in Decline*, New York, Norton.

Herman, E.S. (1982), *The Real Terror Network*, Boston, South End.

Hettne, B. (1983), 'Self reliance and destabilization in the Caribbean and Central America: The cases of Jamaica and Nicaragua', *Scandanavian Journal of Development Alternatives*, March, pp.5–18.

Higgott, R. (1981), 'Beyond the Sociology of Underdevelopment', *Social Analysis* 7, pp.78–98.

Hirsch, F. (1977), *Social Limits to Growth*, London, Routledge and Kegan Paul.

Hunt, E.K. and H.J. Sherman (1972), *Economics*, New York, Harper and Row.

International Union of Food and Allied Workers Associations (1984), 'Experience confirms labours doubts about EPZ's', *News Bulletin* 1, pp.1–3.

Jenkins, R. (1970), *Exploitation*, London, Paladin.

Kaplan, F.M. (1977), *Dubious Spectre: A Second Look at the*

Soviet Threat, Washington, Transnational Institute.

Katznelson, I. and M. Kesselman (1988), *The Politics of Power*.

Kent, G. (1985), 'Food trade: The poor feed the rich', *Ecologist* 15, 5/6.

Kitching, G. (1982), *Development and Underdevelopment in Historical Perspective: Population Nationalism and Industrialization*, London, Methuen.

Klare, M. (1977), *Supplying Repression: US Support for Authoritarian Regimes Abroad*, Institute for Policy Studies.

Kloby, J. (1987), 'The Growing Divide', *Monthly Review*, Sept., 39, 4, pp.1–8.

Kuznets, S. (1966), *Modern Economic Growth: Rate Structure and Spread*, New Haven, Yale University Press.

Kuznets, S. (1968), *Towards a Theory of Economic Growth*, New York, Norton.

Lall, S., and P. Streeten (1977), *Foreign Investment, Transnationals and Developing Countries*, Boulder, Westview Press.

Langmore, J. (1987), 'World trade: A new international (dis)order', *Australian Society*, April.

Lean, G. (1978), *Rich World Poor World*, London, Allen and Unwin.

Lens, S. (1980), 'But can we trust the Russians? The fatal fallacy of the Soviet Threat', *Progressive* 44, 7, July, pp. 19–20.

Lipton, M. (1977), *Why the Poor Stay Poor*, London, Temple Smith.

Loehr, E.G.W. and J.P. Powelson (1981), *The Economies of Development and Distribution*, New York, Harcourt Brace.

Loup, J. (1980), *Can The Third World Survive?*

MacFarlane, S.N. (1985), *Superpower Rivalry and Third World Radicalism*, London, Croom Helm.

McGowan, P.J. and B. Kurdan (1981), 'Imperialism in world system perspective', *International Studies Quarterly* 25, 1, March, pp.43–68.

McGutcheon, R. (1979), *Limits of a Modern World*, London, Butterworths.

Mack, A. (1982), *Is There a Soviet Threat?* Peace Dossier

3, Melbourne, Victorian Association for Peace Studies, July.

Mack, A. and R. Leaver (1981), 'Radical Theories of Development: An Assessment', in A. Mack (ed), *Imperialism, Intervention and Development*, London, Croom Helm, pp.257–285.

McRobie, G. (1981), *Small is Possible*, London, Cape.

Magdoff, H. (1969), *The Age of Imperialism, The Economics of U.S. Foreign Policy*, New York, Monthly Review Press.

Marx, K. (1905), *Capital, Vol 1*, Chicago, Charles Kerr.

Marx, K. (1968), *Communist Manifesto: Selected Works in One Volume*, Karl Marx and Frederick Engels, Lawrence and Wishart.

Mesarovic, M. (1975), *Mankind at the Turning Point*, London, Hutchinson.

Mollison, B. (1979), *Permaculture II*, Stanley, Tasmania, Tagari.

Mollison, B. and D. Holmgren (1978), *Permaculture I*, Hobart, University of Tasmania.

Morawetz, D. (1977), *Twenty Five Years of Economic Development, 1950–1975*, Washington, World Bank.

Morello, T. (1983a), 'The patter of fewer feet', *Far Eastern Economic Review*, 7 July, pp. 33–35.

Morello, T. (1983b) 'Sweatshops in the sun', *Far Eastern Economic Review*, Sept 15.

Muller, R. (1979), 'Poverty is the product', in G. Modelski (ed), *Transnational Corporations and World Order*, San Francisco, Freeman.

Murdoch, W. (1980), *The Poverty of Nations: The Political Economy of Hunger and Population*, Baltimore, Johns Hopkins.

Myers, N. (1987), The kill factor, *The Guardian*, 9th Oct.

Nash, J. (1979), *We Eat the Mines and the Mines Eat Us*, New York, Columbia University Press.

Osterfeld, D. (1982), 'Assessing the New International Order: Prospects for Third World Development', *Journal of Social Political and Economic Studies* 7, 1–2, Spring/ Summer, pp. 3–26.

Park, Y.C. (1981), 'Export-led development: The Korean experience 1960–78', in E. Lee (ed), *Export-led Industrialisation and Development*, I.L.O. Geneva, Ch.4.

Petras, J. (1986), 'Dialectics of growth and regression', *Economic and Political Weekly*, Oct 11, pp.1783–1786.

Piggot, J. (1984), 'The distribution of wealth in Australia – A survey', *Economic Record*, Sept., pp.252–265.

Pilkington, F. (1981), 'Bill Warren and Imperialism', *Journal of Contemporary Asia* 11, 4, pp.159–189.

Polanyi, K. (1985), *The Great Transformation*, Boston, Beacon.

Prins, G. (ed) (1983), *Defended to Death*, Harmondsworth, Penguin.

Raskell, P. (1978), 'Who's got what in Australia: The distribution of wealth', *Journal of Australian Political Economy* 2, June, pp.3–17.

Reutlinger, S. (1977), 'Malnutrition: A poverty or a food problem?' *World Development* 5, 8, pp.715–24.

Rothgeb, J.M. (1984), 'The effects of foreign investment on overall and sectoral growth in Third World states', *Journal of Peace Research* 21, 1, pp.5–16.

Sale, K. (1980), *Human Scale*, Secker and Warberg.

Seligson, M.A. (ed) (1984), *The Gap Between Rich and Poor*, Boulder, Westview.

Sell, R.R. and Kuntz, S.J. (1986), 'Debt, dependency and death: The political economy of mortality in the capitalist world system', *International Sociological Association Conference Paper*.

Sharp, R. and F. Trainer (1984), 'The end or new beginnings?' Chapter 13 in *Apocalypse No!*, Sydney, Pluto, pp.247–287.

Skinner, J.K. (1985), 'Big Mac and the tropical forests', *Monthly Review* 37, 7, Dec., pp.25–32.

Slee, J. (1976), 'State of raw dependence', *Sydney Morning Herald*, 17 May.

Smith, S. (1980), 'The ideas of Samir Amin: Theory or Tautology?', *Journal of Development Studies* 17, 1.

Smith, S. (1982), 'Class analysis vs World Systems:

Critique of Samir Amin's Typology of underdevelopment', *Journal of Contemporary Asia* 12(1).

Sutcliffe, R. (1985), 'Industry and underdevelopment reexamined'. *Journal of Development Studies* 21, 1985/6, pp.121–33.

Thompson, W.R. (ed) (1983), *Contending Approaches to World Systems Analyses*, London, Sage.

Timberlake, L. (1985), *Africa in Crisis*, London, Earthscan.

Todaro, M. (1985), *Economic Development in the Third World*, London, Longman.

Toh, M.S-H. (1986), 'Third World Studies: Conscientization in the Geography Classroom', (Mimeo) Education, University of New England.

Trainer, F.E. (1984), 'The limitations of alternative energy sources', *Conservation and Recycling* 7, 1, pp.27–42.

Trainer, F.E. (1985), *Abandon Affluence!* London, Zed.

Trainer, F.E. (1986a), 'A critical examination of "The Ultimate Resource" and "The Resourceful Earth"', *Technological Forecasting and Social Change* 30, 1, Aug, pp.19–38.

Trainer, F.E. (1986b) *Third World Development: Documents*, (Edited collection) Menzies Library, University of New South Wales, Open Reserve WP0164.

Trainer, F. (1987), 'Peace, Justice, Affluence – Neglected Connections', in D. Green and D. Headon, *Imagining the Real*, Sydney, A.B.C. Enterprises, pp.66–76.

UN Department of Social and Economic Affairs (1975), *The Population Debate*.

UNICEF (1977), 'Hungry Children Eyes', *Development Forum*, Aug–Sept.

UNICEF (1987), *The State of the World's Children: A Statistical Picture*, New York.

United Nations (1976), *Fourth U.N. Conference on Trade and Development*, Geneva.

United Nations (1980), *Food*, Development Issue Paper for the 1980s, II.

Vaitsos, C.V. (1974), *Intercountry Income Distribution and Transnational Enterprise*, Oxford, Clarendon Press.

Waddell, R. (1979), *Technology for Appropriate Development in the Pacific*, Duplicated Manuscript, Dept of Social Studies, University of New South Wales.

Wallerstein, I. (1979), *The Capitalist World Economy*, London, Cambridge University Press.

Warren, Bill (1973), 'Imperialism and capitalist industrialization', *New Left Review* 81, Sept–Oct, pp.3–45.

Warren, Bill (1980), *Imperialism: Pioneer of Capitalism*, London, New Left Books.

Wheelwright, E.L. (1980), 'The new international division of labour in the age of the transnational corporation', in J. Friedman, E.L. Wheelwright and J. Connell, *Development Strategies in the Eighties*, Monograph 1, Development Studies Colloquium, Town and Country Planning, University of Sydney, pp.43–58.

Wolfe, A. (1984), *The Rise and Fall of the Soviet Threat*, Boston, South End.

World Bank (1986), *World Development Report*, London, Oxford University Press.

Worsley, P. (1980), 'One world or three? A critique of the World System Theory of Immanuel Wallerstein', *Socialist Register*, pp.298–338.